Overcoming Hindrances

OS HILLMAN

OVERCOMING HINDRANCES

TO FULFILLING YOUR DESTINY

ASLAN GROUP
PUBLISHING

Aslan Group Publishing

3520 Habersham Club Drive

Cumming, Georgia 30041 USA

678.455.6262

www.AslanGroupPublishing.com

www.marketplaceleaders.org

ISBN-13: 978-1-888582-07-9

Dedication

To all those who acknowledge that we are all pilgrims on a journey toward Christlikeness and that Jesus was the only One who made plan A; for the rest of us, He makes our B plan and C plans His A plan. Thank God He never gives up on us.

Special Acknowledgements

Thank you Kim Bacastow for your proofreading and editing of this work.

A special thanks also to my committed staff — Charis, Monika, Karen, Kim, and René. My team is the best! You are greatly loved and appreciated!

Table of Contents

Foreword   1

Introduction   5

ONE   Overcoming through God's Redemptive Plan   13

TWO   Overcoming Me and the Devil   25

THREE   Overcoming Generational Iniquity and Spirituals Strongholds   35

FOUR   Overcoming Arrested Development and Childhood Wounds   59

FIVE   Overcoming the False-self — Poser   67

SIX   Overcoming by Discovering Your True Self   75

SEVEN   Overcoming Mother-Son Bonding —
         Repairing the Relationship Breach   85

EIGHT   Overcoming the Performance Trap —
         Accepting the Father's Love   105

NINE   Overcoming by Transforming Your Past into a New Identity   119

TEN   Overcoming by Realizing and Contending for your Identity   127

Notes   133

Foreword

Many years ago I realized that every day of our lives there is a spiritual battle over our purpose and destiny. Satan and demonic spirits desire to rob God of "His inheritance in the saints." That's right! God's inheritance is in you and me, the saints. Paul prayed, "that the eyes of your heart may be enlightened, so that you will know what are the riches of the glory of His inheritance in the saints" (Ephesians 1:18). God receives His full inheritance when you and I, not only receive forgiveness of our sins and eternal life, but when we complete the purpose for which the Father placed us on planet earth. I believe that the greatest desire of Satan, who hates God, is to be able to shake his finger in God's face at the end of your life and declare to God, "Ha ha! You received no inheritance in that saint. He was here on the earth for ninety years, but never fulfilled any of the purpose for which You placed him here."

On the other hand, I believe that it is God's great pleasure to be able to say to you at the end of your life, "Well done my daughter! You accomplished your purpose and destiny. You ran the course and fulfilled My calling on your life. I received My full inheritance through your life on earth."

As a result of the devil's desire to steal God's inheritance and your destiny, Satan and the kingdom of darkness begin to work to deceive you and hinder the fulfillment of your destiny from the very beginning of your life. I have found that the enemy takes advantage of us especially during the vulnerable years of our childhood. Many times the enemy uses circumstances and unsuspecting parents to impart from a very early age his message of worthlessness, incompetence, insecurity, and abandonment into the depths of our hearts. When a child is made to feel worthless, incompetent, alone, and like his needs won't be met, these feelings create great fear, insecurity, and lack of peace in his mind and emotions. His "flesh" then goes to work to "do something" to attempt to bring a false sense of peace and security to the mind and emotions.

The Bible tells us in Hebrews 4:10, "For the one who has entered His rest has himself also rested from his works, as God did from His." I have learned that when the enemy imparts one or many deep emotional wounds in childhood that retain the emotions in fear, insecurity, and turmoil, in adult life such a person will not be able to be at rest inside, but rather will constantly be "working" to do something in an attempt to bring value to his life or to meet his own needs. Through this inability to be at rest and "cease from doing our own works," the enemy is then able to effectively hinder us from fulfilling our purpose and destiny. As long as I am not at rest inside and am busy working my own works, God cannot work His works through me.

The types of adult deception and self-sabotaging dysfunction that Os describes in this book, Overcoming Hindrances are exactly the types of manifestations that result from the lack of inner rest in the mind and emotions. The battle then is continually waged by the devil and the kingdom of darkness to keep us from seeing these hidden hindrances, and to thereby rob us of the fulfillment of our destiny. In this book Os will help expose in a very clear way hidden areas of deception and self-sabotage that may even now be hindering the fulfillment of your God-given purpose and destiny. As you read the book, you will find that the truths that are revealed are not just a theory or a teaching, but are real-life hindrances that Os has discovered and continues to work through in his own life.

In Revelation 12:11, speaking of overcoming Satan and the kingdom of darkness, we are told, "they overcame him because of the blood of the Lamb and because of the word of their testimony…" In this book, Overcoming Hindrances to Fulfilling Your Destiny, Os Hillman very candidly and openly shares his own personal journey in overcoming the hindrances in his life. Many teachers are happy to teach principles they have learned from the Bible, but not many are willing to share their own personal battles, victories and failures. The power of this book is not only in the principles taught, but in the testimonies Os shares of his own battles to overcome the hindrances he has faced in his life. I highly recommend this book for anyone, but especially for leaders, who frequently hide behind their talents and accomplishments. May God use the truths in this book to expose and set you free from the hindrances that the enemy has used to block you from fulfilling your purpose and destiny!

Craig Hill
Family Foundations International

"In 25 years of research close to 98% of the issues couples deal with are rooted in childhood wounds each of them suffered below the age of 11." —Dr Paul Hegstrom[1]

Introduction

I was shocked when I first heard this statement. However, after examining the basis for this statement and my own personal experience, I became convinced it was true. Satan's assault on the human race begins at birth. He literally tries to kill you at birth. He tries to kill babies everyday through abortion. He tried to kill Jesus at birth. He tried to kill Moses at birth. Satan's mission statement is found in John 10:10 – to steal, kill and destroy. If he can't kill you at birth, he will try to wound you so badly in childhood that you will grow up dysfunctional because of shame, abuse, neglect, rejection or simply by a lack of nurturing through parental love.

However, the good news is that the truth shall make us free (John 8:32)! Jesus Christ can and will deliver and heal all of us from whatever wounds Satan has inflicted upon our souls.

"The Spirit of the Lord God is upon Me,
Because the Lord has anointed Me
To preach good tidings to the poor;
He has sent Me to heal the brokenhearted,

5

To proclaim liberty to the captives —Isaiah 61:1

As a Christian for more than forty years, I have realized in my own life there have been layers of generational dysfunction that had to be peeled away to discover my true heart and to reveal the truth about the root causes of behavior that contributed to the enemy's scheme to steal, kill and destroy. They often come early in life through a wound in our childhood. These wounds are often never dealt with until the effects of these wounds show up in our adult lives as conflicts in relationships, addictions, or independence designed to protect a wounded heart. Relationship misunderstandings, poor communication and even an unloving spirit are fruits of unresolved pain. Mix in legitimate spiritual warfare from the enemy of our soul whose single mission is to steal, kill and destroy our lives and you have a time bomb simply waiting to explode. Behavior modification is only a band-aid; true healing only happens when you discover and deal with the origin of entry.

I've written this book as a life preserver for those willing to look inside, in hopes that my pain and discoveries might help you uncover the enemy's schemes designed to keep truth hidden so you will not deal with destructive life patterns that destroy relationships close to you and even your relationship with God. Unless we do this our destiny is in jeopardy. We will not fulfill the purpose God intended for our life.

One word of caution is needed before we begin this journey. There are no perfect people on this planet. Jesus is the only person on earth who made plan A in life. For the rest of us, He turns our B and C plan into His A plan. He is a redemptive God. I eventually had to come to a place to realize that no matter how much I worked on myself it may not result in achieving the outcome I desired, especially when others are part of the equation. God gives man free will. People ultimately must make choices that may not be the right choices.

The moment we allow others to define who we are, we make those people a god and an idol in our lives. Let's face it; hurt people, hurt people.

God always looks past our failures to see our potential. When God spoke to Gideon, He said, "Oh, warrior!" He was not looking at his past or current status. He was seeing what Gideon was to become. We must see others for what God wants them to become. Shame and performance keeps people locked into their past.

Sometimes those we hurt get stuck in their hurt and disappointment and lose their will to fight. They conclude it is a losing battle. Until God also does the deeper work in their lives it is difficult for healing to take place. We are all responsible for our own behavior. Discovering roots of behavior allows us to move toward change. However, some people will not allow us the freedom to fail so that we can change. Performance creates more bondage; unconditional love gives people freedom to fail and

> The moment we allow others to define who we are, we make those people a god and an idol in our lives.

ultimately leads to freedom and success. Some who see themselves as the victim give up before the victory is won, losing the opportunity to attain what they always wanted. Someone once said the hardest place to score a touchdown from is the one yard line. The darkest part of a night is just before sunrise.

The greatest gift a person can give to another is unconditional love. When those who know you the most still love you the most, this fosters the freedom to change. This does not mean tough love with appropriate boundaries is not needed in the process. However, I have seen where some who play the victim actually keep their offender in bondage to their past by not allowing them the freedom to change. They sabotage relationship healing because of their own unresolved pain through their control and manipulation. They refuse to believe God can do that deeper work in their loved one, thereby living the victim role.

The Gadarene Demoniac

The story of the Gadarene demoniac is a story of redemption. Here is a man filled with demons. Read his story.

> *Then they sailed to the country of the Gadarenes, which is opposite Galilee. And when He stepped out on the land, there met Him a certain man from the city who had demons for a long time. And he wore no clothes, nor did he live in a house but in the tombs. When he saw Jesus, he cried out, fell down before Him, and with a loud voice said, "What have I to do with You, Jesus, Son of the Most High God? I beg You, do not torment me!",For He had commanded the unclean spirit to come out of the man. For it had often seized him, and he was kept under guard, bound with chains and shackles; and he broke the bonds and was driven by the demon into the wilderness.*
>
> *Jesus asked him, saying, "What is your name?"*
>
> *And he said, "Legion," because many demons had entered him. And they begged Him that He would not command them to go out into the abyss.*
>
> *Now a herd of many swine was feeding there on the mountain. So they begged Him that He would permit them to enter them. And He permitted them.*

*Then the demons went out of the man and entered the
swine, and the herd ran violently down the steep place
into the lake and drowned.*

*When those who fed them saw what had happened,
they fled and told others in the city and throughout
the country. They came out to see what had happened.
They found the man from whom the demons had
departed, sitting at the feet of Jesus, clothed and in his
right mind. And they were afraid. They asked them by
what means he who had been demon-possessed was
healed. Then the whole multitude of the surrounding
region of the Gadarenes asked Him to depart from
them, for they were seized with great fear. And He got
into the boat and returned.*

*Now the man from whom the demons had depart-
ed begged Him that he might be with Him. But Jesus
sent him away, saying, **"Return to your own house,
and tell what great things God has done for you."**
And he went his way and proclaimed throughout the
whole city what great things Jesus had done for him.*
—Luke 8:38-40

Perhaps the analogy today might be a person who is a drug
addict, an abuser, a homosexual, an adulterer or maybe he is
simply a work-a-holic who neglects his family. How much does
one have to believe in redemption to free a life that is still controlled by demons? At what point do we walk away?

Jesus NEVER believes a human being is hopeless. When we
decide to give up on a person we have become judge and jury
in the life of that person. We make a judgment. God says when
we judge, we too, will be judged. "Judge not, that you be not
judged. For with what judgment you judge, you will be judged;

and with the measure you use, it will be measured back to you" (Matthew 7:1-2).

God's nature is faithfulness in the face of unfaithfulness. He is a God of covenant. His love and commitment to me is not dependent on my performance, but upon my heart response to Him. Your greatest assignment and privilege in the life of the sinner is to give up your life just as Jesus gave up His for us. Jesus challenged those who wanted to condemn the prostitute by saying, "You who have no sin cast the first stone." Being a

> When we decide to give up on a person we have become judge and jury in the life of that person.

judge of others is the height of self-righteousness and pride. God calls us to stand in the gap for others (Ezekiel 22:30). Our life is not our own.

The Gadarene man may have had a family. Was there a wife and family to go back to? Or, had she moved on? Sometimes we simply cannot wait for God's timing to do His deeper work in those who caused pain in our lives. We choose the self-righteous, victim role. Our pride says, "I've waited long enough. He/she had their chance." Then, later we learn of the wonderful work God has done. But, now it is too late. You've moved on because you could not trust God for this person. You wrongly believed he or she was beyond God's reach.

People will always want to define us based on our past or even present behavior; however, God sees our future; He sees who we are becoming. There is a place for measurable account-ability, but this must be balanced with grace, forgiveness and a deep realization that we are all sinners in need of the healing and forgiveness of God and from those who are willing to live in covenant with us. And, we must forgive ourselves too. We cannot begin to love others if we do not love ourselves. Shame and performance keep people in bondage; forgiveness frees them to become more like Jesus.

If David could not have discovered these truths, he would surely have spent years in prison as a murdering adulterer. Instead, God saw a man willing to work on his weaknesses, many that were probably a result of childhood wounds. He failed, but he learned from his failures. Proverbs calls this man a "simple fool", one who makes a mistake but learns from them. No other Bible character had more chapters written about his life than David — over 70! That's because God always looks at the heart, not just performance.

The things I share in this book have, in many cases, affected me at a personal level in my life. By sharing these with you my hope is you will experience freedom to overcome all your hindrances and to discover Satan's strategies he seeks to employ against you to defeat you so you cannot fulfill God's ultimate destiny for your life. And, more importantly, you will discover the depth of His love He has for you and me.

> People will always want to define us based on our past or even present behavior; however, God sees our future; He sees who we are becoming.

Os Hillman

*...for the Son of Man
has come to seek
and to save that
which was lost.*
—Luke 19:10

ONE

Overcoming through God's Redemptive Plan

Do you believe God is in control?

I often ask this question when I'm speaking to audiences. More than half the audience will raise their hands in agreement that they believe God is in control. However, let me propose to you that God is not in control.

Yes, God is omnipotent and omnipresent and He can do anything He wants to do any time He wants to do it. In fact, the Bible says in Psalm 135:6 "Whatever the Lord pleases He does, in heaven and in earth."

However, God has chosen to work through human beings, which means that much of the activity on earth will only be accomplished if human beings cooperate with God through prayer, intercession and obedience to His commands. He exerts limited authority over the earth because He has delegated authority to man through Jesus Christ.

When God created earth He also created Adam and Eve. The world was sinless and the relationship between God and

13

man was perfect. All their needs were met through their relationship with God. God gave dominion over the entire earth to Adam and Eve. Then God said, "Let Us make man in Our image, according to Our likeness; let them have dominion over the fish of the sea, over the birds of the air, and over the cattle, over all the earth and over every creeping thing that creeps on the earth" (Genesis 1:26). They had an intimate relationship with their Heavenly Father until Adam and Eve decided that God was holding out on them.

When Adam and Eve sinned, the world changed forever. No longer did they have the intimate relationship with their Heavenly Father. Sin broke the Father-son/daughter relationship. They were now slaves and orphans and residents of a global orphanage.

The Bible says that when Satan came into the world he was now considered by Jesus "ruler of the world" (John 12:21). Jesus tells us that Satan was ruler of the world in three different places in the book of John.

> When God thinks of you, love swells in his heart.

God took a huge risk when He gave man free will. By giving man free will it meant that God would be blamed for many things that Satan would do. By giving man free will He knew that evil would work through man and man would blame God for the evil instead of Satan, who is the author of evil.

This is why so many unbelievers ask the question, "If God is a God of love, then how could the Holocaust happened? Why do good people suffer?" Certainly this is always the question we ask when things take place we cannot resolve in our minds. We start down a slippery slope of impugning the nature of God when we begin attributing evil to God.

This is what happened to Cain in Genesis when he impugned the nature of God because God judged his attitude regarding his sacrifice. God did not reject Cain; He rejected his attitude and motivation for his sacrifice. Cain impugned the nature of God by accusing God of rejecting him; it was his attitude toward his sacrifice, not God's rejection of him, that allowed the spirit of rejection to turn into bitterness that led to murdering his own brother.

God is Love

We know that God is love because the scripture tells us that God is love. Zephaniah 3:17 tells us "The Lord your God is in your midst, the mighty one, will save; He will rejoice over you with gladness, He will quiet you with His love, He will rejoice over you with singing."

You see, when God thinks of you, love swells in his heart. There's nothing you can do that will change the love the Father has for you. Yes, you impact that relationship by sinning. But, His love will never change and there is always an open door to repentance and re-establishment of that relationship based on 1 John 1:9: "If we confess our sins, He is faithful and just to forgive us our sins and to cleanse us from all unrighteousness."

God decided that He wanted to restore His relationship with man. So, He decided to send His only Son to earth to pay for man's sin. This, too, is further proof of the deep love God, the Father has for man. It says in Luke 19:10 that Jesus came to reclaim all **that** had been lost. "That" means that Jesus came to restore everything that had been lost as a result of man's sin in the garden. That included their relationship with God, their relationship to their work life, their relationship to each other and much more.

When Jesus was crucified for you and me He accomplished several things. He told His disciples that he was going to delegate all of his authority on earth to His disciples and us as His representative. He said in Matthew 16:19: "And I will give you the keys of the kingdom of heaven, and whatever you bind on earth will be bound in heaven, and whatever you loose on earth will be loosed in heaven." He also told us that after He left they would do even greater works than He did on the earth because they would soon receive the power the Holy Spirit: "Most assuredly, I say to you, he who believes in Me, the works that I do he will do also; and greater works than these he will do, because I go to My Father" (John 14:12).

In Ezekiel 22:30 we read what God is looking for from man today. "So I looked for a man among them who would make a wall, and stand in the gap before Me on behalf of the land, so that I should not destroy it; but I found no one." In essence, He is asking, "Is anyone willing to stand on behalf of the culture so that He would not have to destroy it?" "He saw that there was no man, and wondered that there was no intercessor" (Isaiah 59:16).

God chooses to work through human beings. He rarely works outside of human beings. Yes, it does happen. However, he generally chooses to work through human beings. That's why when you're awakened in the middle of the night to pray for someone, God is actually looking for someone He can use to pray a prayer that is already His will to answer. God is looking for someone to be the vessel to accomplish something He wants to do, but He needs a human being to pray it into existence. You and I are His representatives. So what we need to learn is how we are to fulfill the purposes of God on earth.

My good friend Craig Hill shares a powerful story of this principle that God is looking for someone to pray His will on planet earth. It was six months before Craig met Jan, his future wife. They learned a powerful lesson about how God answers prayer.

In early 1975, Craig had just graduated from college and had a nine-month period of time before he would start a two year graduate MBA program in Chicago. For the first few months of the year, Craig was employed as a co-pilot in a Learjet flying the U.S. mail out of Grand Rapids, Michigan five nights a week. He would leave Grand Rapids around midnight and fly to Chicago, Bloomington, Illinois and on to St. Louis. Then he would fly back to Peoria, Illinois, Chicago again and then back across Lake Michigan to Grand Rapids.

One night, on the last leg of the trip from Chicago back to Grand Rapids, the Chicago air traffic control center advised Craig that the weather in much of Michigan was deteriorating very rapidly and had very limited visibility. They suggested that he might want to return to Chicago.

The captain and he looked at each other, and he asked him, "Do you want to go back to Chicago?"

"No," I answered. "If we do, we will probably get stuck in the pilot's lounge all day. I'm tired. I want to go home and go to bed. I bet we can beat the fog into Grand Rapids."

He concurred with Craig. They told the air-traffic control that they would continue to Grand Rapids.

Craig said, "I don't know why, but I have noticed that frequently they locate airports right in the crook of a river. This is the case in Grand Rapids, Michigan. So where does the fog form first? Right over the river, of course, which is right on the approach into the precision-instrument approach runway. As a result, we discovered that when the visibility was low, many times we could get into the airport on the non-precision instrument approach from the non-river end of the runway more easily even though the visibility and altitude minimums were higher than they were from the other direction.

This particular night, we shot the first instrument approach with no success. When we arrived at the minimum altitude we saw no runway come, no lights, no ground; nothing but fog. So we ascended and tried to precision approach from the other direction. On dissent on the second approach, two little red lights illuminated on our panel, "low fuel."

Unfortunately, the second approach yielded the same results as the first. Now they both knew that they had made a mistake. They asked the controllers what was the closest airport with above visibility minimums. They responded that Lansing, Michigan was still open.

So they headed for Lansing as fast as they could go. Unfortunately, with the type of jet engines that powered this Learjet, they were burning at low altitude about four times as much fuel as we burned at cruise altitude. When they arrived at Lansing, they again shot an instrument approach from each of two directions to the minimum altitude, but the fog was already too thick to allow them to see the runway lights. Now they were really low on fuel. They asked the controller what other airport near them was open. They sent them to Detroit but added that the visibility was going down fast there, too.

Craig was now beginning to really fear for his life. As they flew over to Detroit, he was having visions of Heaven and talking with the saints of old. He could just see himself conversing with a Abraham, Moses, and Peter.

"And how did you die, Peter?" I was queried.

"Well," he said, "I was crucified upside down for the name of Christ. And how did you die, Craig?"

"I was stupid and ran out of fuel in an airplane," I reluctantly had to admit. I really did not want to have that testimony for all of eternity.

When they finally arrived in Detroit, they were the second to the last airplane to make it into the Detroit airport before the fog reduced the visibility below minimums at that airport also. They landed with literally only minutes of fuel left.

Later in July of that year, Craig met Jan on the team in Europe. Through the autumn of that year he continued to meet at Jan's parent's home every third weekend or so. During this time of getting to know each other, Craig was relating to Jan the various "heroic" adventures of his life. One evening at her parent's home, Craig was sharing with her how he had almost run out of fuel and crashed in a Learjet in Michigan earlier that year. As the story unfolded, a surprised look came upon Jan's face and as he finished, she remarked, "I have to ask you two questions."

"What are those? "he replied.

"Was the other guy quite a bit older than you?"

"Yes." he replied.

"Were you both wearing light blue, one-piece flight suits?"

"Yes," he replied. "But why would you ask that question?"

"We prayed for you!" she announced.

"What do you mean, "You prayed for me?" "This happened in January. I didn't even meet you until July. How could you have prayed for me when you didn't even know me yet?"

Then Jan began to explain. At that time in January 1975, Jan had been part of the Youth With a Mission (YWAM) school of evangelism in Germany. Every morning the students met in small groups for prayer. During the course of the school, the intercessor Bible teacher, Joy Dawson, talked to the students about a particular prayer model. Usually when people pray, they simply pray for their "shopping list" of all the things that they would like God to help them with. They just pray for the things that are important to them.

In this YWAM school Joy Dawson had taught the students to ask the Lord "What was on His heart that day that He would like them to pray. It was their understanding that they were to partner with God in prayer to release His authority on earth to accomplish his purposes.

Consequently, every morning in their small groups of students they would first ask the Lord what He wanted them to pray about. They would listen for the topic that came to their minds with each other and make a list of these topics. They then proceeded to take each topic one by one and ask the Lord what they were to pray. Frequently, the Holy Spirit would bring to their minds things to pray which they had no natural cognitive knowledge.

Sometimes they would receive confirmation from natural sources regarding the things that they prayed,

*but most times they could not. Each day they were
simply faithful to pray what God spoke to them.*

*Jan shared with Craig that one day back in January
they were asking God for what they would pray
for that day, one of the topics that came up was that
they were to pray for an airplane. As they prayed
through the list of topics they had for the morning, as
was their custom, when they came to the topic "airplane", they naturally asked the Lord, "What are we
supposed to pray about an airplane?"*

*Then one by one each member of the group shared
and prayed what came to their minds regarding this topic.*

*One person said, "I sense that the airplane we are
to pray for is very small, but very fast like 'United' US
airline company."*

*Another one contributed, "I sense that there are
only two pilots on board. One is old and one is young."*

*Someone else said, "I see that the two pilots are
both wearing light blue one-piece flight suits and they
are carrying the US mail."*

*Jan shared, "I am seeing a map picture of the
western part of the Great Lakes area of United States.
The map appears very dark and is growing foggier. I
believe the plane is running out of gas, we need to
pray for them to find a place to land."*

*The group then proceeded to pray for this airplane for
a safe place to land. They prayed until they felt like the
Holy Spirit had exhausted everything they were to pray for
regarding this topic and the job was complete. They then
went on to the next topic, which was China, or something
that seemed more important in the Kingdom of God.*

Jan further related to Craig that she would not have remembered this specific instance of prayer, as they pray for things for which they had no natural knowledge of every day. So, this day was not particularly notable.

However, after the prayer time that day, another one of the students who was a member of that small-group approached Jan and told her, "Jan, I sensed that the airplane we prayed for has something to do with you." Jan thought for a moment and then replied, "I don't really know anyone who is involved with airplanes. I am from a small town in Iowa. It was a farmer I knew who had a small airplane, which I heard he sometimes flew in and out of his cornfield. But I really don't think it has anything to do with him. I really can't think of anyone else right now."

The girl in the group said, "Well, I don't know. I just sense that I was supposed to tell you that."[2]

What this powerful story tells us is that everything changes once we understand that prayer is not about trying to get God to listen to me, but it is about God trying to get me to listen to Him to be His representative on the earth to enforce His covenants.

When Jesus, the ultimate landlord, returns to the earth He will take back everything He leased to us on earth. We will no longer be responsible for planet earth after He returns. But in the meantime, we need to understand how to defeat the works of Satan. The Bible tells us this was one of Jesus' primary missions. "He who sins is of the devil, for the devil has sinned from the beginning. For this purpose the Son of God was manifested, that He might destroy the works of the devil" (John 3:8).

When Jesus left the earth that assignment was passed to us. "Go therefore and make disciples of all the nations, baptizing them in the name of the Father and of the Son and of the Holy Spirit, teaching them to observe all things that I have commanded you; and lo, I am with you always, even to the end of the age" (Matthew 28:19-21).

In order for you to fulfill your destiny, you must understand the authority God placed within you. You must understand how important you are to fulfilling God's purposes on the earth.

For more on Satan's lies, see our three free videos at www.3greatestlies.com.

Questions for Reflection and Discussion

1. Is God in control? Explain the concept of delegated authority.

2. How do we impugn the nature of God? Have you ever attributed evil to God? Explain.

3. Read Ezekiel 22:30. Explain this verse in the context of prayer.

For we who live are always delivered to death for Jesus' sake, that the life of Jesus also may be manifested in our mortal flesh. So then death is working in us, but life in you.
—2 Corinthians 4:11-12

Overcoming Me and the Devil

Both God and Satan want you dead, but each for different reasons. God wants to kill your flesh in order that the life of Jesus will be revealed through you to others. Satan wants to kill you. He wants to kill your destiny. Satan tried to kill Moses at birth; and he tried to kill Jesus at birth. He tries to kill all of us through abortion. But if he can't kill us, then he will try to wound us through broken families and dysfunctional parenting. He wants to wound you so badly in childhood that you will grow up dysfunctional so that you will not be able to relate to God and others in a healthy way. Ultimately, he wants you and me to be messed up, wounded individuals throughout our life.

Satan's mission statement is revealed in John 10:10 which says that he came to steal, kill, and destroy through his false prophets. I like to say that Satan wants to steal your money, kill your destiny, and destroy your family. That is his mission. The name Satan means "Opposer".

Know Thy Enemy; Know Thyself

In team sports a scouting report must be conducted to evaluate the strengths and weaknesses of your opponent. If you know your opponent you will know how to prepare your team for what they will face. You can prepare for how they will play

against you. Knowing the truth about their capabilities, not just what they say their capabilities are, will allow you to prepare. This is true in the spiritual world, too. We must understand

> Satan's mission statement is to steal, kill, and destroy

Satan's strategy he uses against us.

Many people today simply do not believe in a literal Satan. The apostle Paul clearly understood there was an unseen demonic world when he penned these words.

> *"Finally, be strong in the Lord and in His mighty power. Put on the full armor of God so that you can take your stand against the devil's schemes. For our struggle is not against flesh and blood, but against the rulers, against the authorities, against the powers of this dark world and against the spiritual forces of evil in the heavenly realms. Therefore put on the full armor of God, so that when the day of evil comes, you may be able to stand your ground, and after you have done everything, to stand" (Ephesians 6:10-13). He re-enforced this when he said, "For a great and effective door has opened to me, and there are many adversaries" (1 Corinthians 16: 9).*

George Barna Research has found that only 24% of the general population believes Satan is a real being and amazingly, only 52% of Christians believe Satan is real.[3] C.S. Lewis said, "There are two mistakes the church makes when dealing with the devil: to blame everything on him or to blame nothing on him." C.S. Lewis wrote a book entitled, The Screwtape Letters. It was a fictional story about a chief demon, Screwtape, and his underling. "I wonder if you should ask me whether it is essential to keep the patient in ignorance of your own existence. That question, at least for the present phase of the struggle, has been answered for us by the High Command. Our policy, for the moment, is to conceal ourselves." Satan wants to keep you in the dark regarding his existence and his schemes.[4]

Following are some ways Satan seeks to destroy humans.

He accuses believers

> Then I heard a loud voice saying in heaven, "Now salvation, and strength, and the kingdom of our God, and the power of His Christ have come, for the accuser of our brethren, who accused them before our God day and night, has been cast down" (Revelation 12:10-11).

He blinds unbelievers

> "But even if our gospel is veiled, it is veiled to those who are perishing, whose minds the god of this age has blinded, who do not believe, lest the light of the gospel of the glory of Christ, who is the image of God, should shine on them" (2 Corinthians 4:3).

He is an angel of light

> "And no wonder! For Satan himself transforms himself into an angel of light" (2 Corinthians 11:14). Some people are used by Satan, posing as Christians but their motives are not for the Kingdom of God.

He seeks to kill and destroy

"The thief does not come except to steal, and to kill, and to destroy. I have come that they may have life, and that they may have it more abundantly" (John 10:10). He wants to steal your money, kill your destiny and destroy your family.

He deceives and lies

"You are of your father the devil, and the desires of your father you want to do. He was a murderer from the beginning, and does not stand in the truth, because there is no truth in him. When he speaks a lie, he speaks from his own resources, for he is a liar and the father of it" (John 8:44).

He wars against those who obey

"And the dragon was enraged with the woman, and he went to make war with the rest of her offspring, who keep the commandments of God and have the testimony of Jesus Christ" (Revelation 12:17).

He is like a lion who seeks to devour

"Be sober, be vigilant; because your adversary the devil walks about like a roaring lion, seeking whom he may devour" (1 Peter 5:8).

He seeks to kill

"His tail drew a third of the stars of heaven and threw them to the earth. And the dragon stood before the woman who was ready to give birth, to devour her Child as soon as it was born" (Revelation 12:4).

4444

Satan's 3 Greatest Lies

These are the 3 main lies Satan wants you to believe. He wants you to believe that you are 1) powerless over your circumstances, 2) you are a victim of an unjust God and 3) He left you here to suffer. If he can make you believe these 3 lies he knows you will impugn God's nature.

Jesus told His disciples that "You're all going to feel that your world is falling apart and that it's my fault" (Mark 14:27 MSG).

> Satan wants you to believe that you are powerless over your circumstances, that you are a victim of an unjust God and that He left you here to suffer.

You see, our lifelong journey in life is a long and brutal assault on our hearts by Satan who knows what we can become and he desperately fears it. He knows that if you become all God created you to be, you will defeat him. He knows you would express the love and power of God through your life and impact many others for God's Kingdom. The Good News is that Jesus came to set all people free and that the truth is what sets us free –"And you shall know the truth, and the truth shall make you free" (John 8:32).

In chapter one I shared that God is looking for a man to represent Him on planet earth. "So I sought for a man among them who would make a wall, and stand in the gap before Me on behalf of the land, that I should not destroy it; but I found no one" (Ezekiel 22:30). In essence, God is asking, "Is anyone willing to stand on behalf of the culture so that He should not have to destroy it?"

This concept can be exemplified by the power of attorney. If you have the power of attorney you have the legal right to represent someone's interest on their behalf. If you have the power of attorney for Bill Gates, you could walk in a bank and cash a

$1 billion check because you have all legal rights to everything that he owns.

Jesus has given you and me power of attorney on his behalf to represent more than 7,500 covenant promises on the earth that are included in the Bible. A covenant promise is an IOU written by God himself that says "I give you the legal right to enforce this covenant upon the earth." What that means is that you and I must be the conduit for God to use on planet earth to pray His covenant promises into reality.

When Jesus, the ultimate Landlord, returns to the earth He will take back everything He has leased to us on earth. We will no longer be responsible for planet earth after He returns. But in the meantime, we need to understand how to defeat the works of Satan.

We, like Paul, must overcome ourselves

Whenever I conduct my Change Agent workshop I often use video clips to illustrate a key principle. During my session on strongholds I share a humorous video clip showing a dog that growls at his own foot. He growls at his foot, thinking his foot is going to attack him. This clip illustrates an important truth. Many times we are our own worst enemy.

When you and I were born-again our spirits were 100% cleansed by the Spirit of God. What Jesus did on the cross provided free access to the Father. Our spirits were immediately aligned with God's Spirit. However, our soul is a different matter. A human being is made up of spirit, soul and body. Within the soul we have our mind, will and emotions. Whenever we come to Christ our soul is not instantly made in the likeness of Jesus. This happens progressively through sanctification. Sanctification is the act or process of acquiring sanctity, of being made or becoming holy. The apostle Paul addressed this when he said, "Now may the

God of peace Himself sanctify you entirely and may your spirit and soul and body be preserved complete without blame at the coming of the Lord Jesus Christ" (1 Thessalonians 5:23).

The apostle Paul understood that the soul still desires to sin. "For what I will to do, that I do not practice; but what I hate, that I do. If, then, I do what I will not to do, I agree with the law that it is good. But now, it is no longer I who do it, but sin that dwells in me" (Romans 7:15-17). Commentators tell us that when Paul wrote Romans he had been a Christian many years. He himself still struggled with doing things that he did not want to do. So, too, do you and I.

God allows us to discover our flesh in order to discover the truth about our condition. His desire for each of us is to crucify our flesh so that Christ can freely live through us. "I have been crucified with Christ; it is no longer I who live, but Christ lives in me; and the life which I now live in the flesh I live by faith in the Son of God, who loved me and gave Himself for me" (Galatians 2:20).

The Pitfalls of Meeting our own Needs

Adam and Eve perceived that God was holding out on them. Satan convinced them that their needs were not being met by God. So, they chose to meet their own needs by disobeying God. They ate from the tree of good and evil. When we seek to meet needs in our own way habits are formed to meet those needs. Sometimes those habits can turn into addictions. An addiction is anything you cannot willingly stop. Henry Wright, author of Addictions, says that addictions are rooted in the need to be loved and a belief that we do not believe we are loved by God. They are counterfeit flesh desires for love and intimacy met through our soul. And they become isolation chambers designed to mask the pain.

There are physiological factors that exist in our brain that lead to addictions. The brain is made up of neurotransmitters in the nervous system. Brainstems in the nervous system emit feel-good hormones. When negative events happen in our lives that cause painful emotions, this causes an under secretion of two neurotransmitters called dopamine and serotonin. When levels of these neurotransmitters become low, depression, anxiety and emotional pain can increase. At that point we are vulnerable to making choices outside God's perfect plan for us. God desires to meet every need in our lives. But when a need arises that we perceive God is not meeting, and it causes emotional pain in our lives and Satan tempts us to meet our own need. And this is how we develop habits that lead to addictions.

> Addictions are rooted in the need to be loved and a belief that we do not believe we are loved by God.

The neurotransmitter dopamine and serotonin act as chemical messengers that relay nerve signals to the brain. Dopamine regulates muscle movement, motivation, and the sensation of pleasure. Serotonin primarily affects mood, impulsiveness and social behaviors.

For instance, when a man is feeling empty, alone, unloved and sensual he may choose pornography to satisfy that need instead of going to God. His real need is to know and experience the Father's love. However, his life is void of true intimacy with God. He does not believe he is loved by God and seeks to deal with his emptiness and pain through his flesh.[5]

Craig Hill, author of Bondage Broken, says most people believe four lies that keep them in bondage to addictions: (1) They believe God is not faithful, (2) They believe the addictive habit will satisfy their need, (3) They believe the habit is stronger than the power of God to defeat it and (4) They believe the addiction is simply the way they are.[6]

If you struggle with addiction let me encourage you to focus your attention on asking the Father to reveal His love to you. Meditate on scriptures related to the love of the Father. I suggest you read my book Experiencing the Father's Love and Listening to the Father's Heart. Once you discover the truth of God's love for you and begin to believe it and experience it you will begin to see your addiction defeated. Healing will be a by-product of experiencing the love of the Father. Sometimes these struggles remain in our soul realm because of generational iniquity. We will address this topic in our next chapter.

I encourage you to watch the three free videos we produced on understanding Satan's lies and how you can defeat them (www.3GreatestLies.com).

Questions for Reflection and Discussion

1. The Bible says we live in a spiritual world with unseen demonic forces. Do you believe this? Share a personal experience where you experienced spiritual warfare.

2. What happens to you when you don't feel God has met a need in your life? How do you meet your need?

3. Addictions are rooted in the belief that God does not love me. Explain what happens physically when we don't feel loved.

The weapons we fight with are not the weapons of the world. On the contrary, they have divine power to demolish strongholds. We demolish arguments and every pretension that sets itself up against the knowledge of God, and we take captive every thought to make it obedient to Christ.
—2 Corinthians 10:4-5

Overcoming Generational Iniquity and Spiritual Strongholds

he apostle Paul enlists the word "stronghold" to define the spiritual fortresses where Satan and his legions go for protection. These fortresses exist in the thought-patterns and ideas that govern individuals in their homes, workplaces and churches, as well as in communities and nations. Before victory can be claimed, these strongholds must be pulled down. Only then can the mighty weapons of the Word and the Spirit effectively plunder Satan's house.

Here is an example of how a stronghold can develop and affect someone's working life. "Jerry" had grown up with a father who was successful and a workaholic. Although Jerry lacked for nothing materially, his parents failed to nurture him with words and healthy physical affection during his growing up years. As an adult he felt a lack of closeness to those around him, especially his wife and kids. He had difficulty sharing his feelings with others. When Jerry was still in his early teens, his father died very suddenly. The insurance failed to pay the life insurance through a complication and his large family was left with little support. Insecurity and fear became the dominating factors in the young man's life.

He recalls his mother often saying after he expressed a financial need: "We don't have enough the money for that." Vowing to himself that he would never again suffer financial need, Jerry worked hard at his business in his adult life, putting stress on many personal and business relationships. He became very successful. He came to faith in Christ in his early twenties.

> Whenever we seek to meet one or more basic needs outside God's design, we set the stage for the development of a generational stronghold caused by generational iniquity.

Jerry became a business owner in his late thirties. His relationship with God was seen as a model among his peers, but when examined closer, there was something that just wasn't right. He often displayed anger in financial situations and he would shame his employees into correcting their behaviors if they failed to perform to his standards. Jerry had little accountability beyond his clients. A pattern began to emerge that motivated Jerry to place restrictions on those around him when they failed in the financial area. Jerry was very independent and was often seen as aloof. It was hard to get "close" to Jerry. Finally, Jerry's marriage disintegrated and some major crises in his business led to financial difficulties.

However, through the counsel of some trusted friends who had an understanding of spiritual strongholds, Jerry came to realize that underneath some of these symptoms, a spiritual stronghold of insecurity and fear had been established that originated in his early childhood. To reduce his anxiety level, Jerry had worked hard to control people and circumstances.

Jerry began to understand the root causes of his behavior and even his independent spirit. As the Holy Spirit convicted him of sins he had committed against people in his life, Jerry sought forgiveness and made restitution. His priorities shifted to developing deeper relationships with God and family first, followed by close friends and business. God began to show Jerry that he could have true intimacy with God and others when these underlying strongholds were removed. Jerry became a new person, and for the first time in his life Jerry experienced a degree of intimacy and freedom in his walk with God. He learned to relate to his Heavenly Father as a son instead of an orphan. He was discovering his true heart for the first time. Today, Jerry sees the hand of God restoring all aspects of his life and can testify to God's miraculous hand in many of his everyday experiences in life and work.

I am pleased to tell you that I am Jerry. It is from first-hand experience that I can discuss the effect of generational iniquity that can plague our lives.

Dealing with Generational Iniquity

By reading between the lines in the first two chapters of Genesis, as well as elsewhere in the Bible, we find that God created us with seven needs: (1) dignity, (2) authority, (3) blessing and provision, (4) security, (5) purpose and meaning, (6) freedom and boundaries, and (7) love and companionship. Whenever we seek to meet one or more of these basic needs outside God's design, we set the stage for the development of a generational stronghold caused by generational iniquity.

"You shall not bow down to them nor serve them. For I, the LORD your God, am a jealous God, visiting the **iniquity** of the fathers upon the children to the third and fourth generations of those who hate Me..." (Deuteronomy 5:9). The Bible speaks of generational iniquity. Sometimes people use the term sin and iniquity in the same way, but they are two different things. Iniquity is not sin, but the root or motivation behind sin. It can be carried down generationally three and four generations. That is why people say that if your father was an alcoholic, you better beware that you, too, will be susceptible to a similar addiction. Iniquity can cause sin and a stronghold to develop in a life.

We must identify and deal with sins that may be rooted in generational iniquity. The following passages reveal the need to confess the iniquity of our fathers. When we do this, we receive forgiveness, healing and restoration. We close the door to future generations that would receive this iniquity if we close the door through repentance.

> But if they confess their iniquity and the iniquity of their fathers, with their unfaithfulness in which they were unfaithful to Me, and that they also have walked contrary to Me, and that I also have walked contrary to them and have brought them into the land of their enemies; if their uncircumcised hearts are humbled, and they accept their guilt— then I will remember My covenant with Jacob, and My covenant with Isaac and My covenant with Abraham I will remember; I will remember the land (Leviticus 26:40-42).

> Please let Your ear be attentive and Your eyes open, that You may hear the prayer of Your servant which I pray before You now, day and night, for the children of Israel Your servants, and confess the sins of the children of Israel which we have sinned against You. Both my father's house and I have sinned (Nehemiah 1:6).

*Then those of Israelite lineage separated themselves
from all foreigners; and they stood and confessed their
sins and the iniquities of their fathers (Nehemiah 9:2).*

God wants to release the full measure of His love in our lives,
so that we close the door to generational iniquity. In Ephesians
3:16-18, Paul prayed that we would experience this fullness:

*I pray that out of His glorious riches He may
strengthen you with power through his Spirit in your
inner being, so that Christ may dwell in your hearts
through faith. And I pray that you, being rooted and
established in love, may have power, together with all
the saints, to grasp how wide and long and high and
deep is the love of Christ, and to know this love that
surpasses knowledge—that you may be filled to the
measure of all the fullness of God.*

I discovered that generational iniquity leads to spiritual
strongholds. It's the root. When I came into a greater understanding of the operation of spiritual strongholds, I did a thor-
ough study of my family history. I interviewed family members
to see what I could learn about the way my father and grand-
father related to God and their families. I studied their work
habits. I found that each of us had the same symptoms:

- A need for recognition from performance (civic projects, sports, business success)
- An emphasis on building financial security (we were
  workaholics)
- A lack of emotional intimacy and ability to live from
  the heart

- A works-based relationship toward God
- A tendency to over-control people and circumstances
- An inability to express words and affection to loved ones

This was an amazing discovery for me. For the first time, I realized this stronghold had affected three generations of my family. I was being given the opportunity to break this generational stronghold through the power of Christ so that it would not get passed down any further.

A woman is freed from rejection

Several years ago I was in Singapore speaking at a marketplace conference. I had just shared my teaching on spiritual strongholds with the conference attendees. A woman ran up to me after the program and asked (or should I say demanded) that I have lunch with her and her friend. She was extremely aggressive and I happened to notice that she was a bit overweight.

We proceeded to lunch. I turned to my new friend and said, "Could you tell me what type of relationship you have with your dad?"

"Why would you want to know that?"

"Well, I'm just curious."

"Well, I have a really bad relationship with my dad. He says I'll never amount to anything!"

I turned to her and began to share that she had a stronghold of rejection operating in her life. She was living her life to try to gain approval from her dad. Her aggressive nature and performance was a symptom of her drivenness to gain success so that she might gain her father's approval.

Subconsciously she had to succeed at all costs. Even her weight was a form of sabotage for the words spoken over her by her dad.

She was the ultimate orphan looking for a father who would love and accept her. She was living as a slave to a performance demon. I told her that God loved her as his own daughter just the way she was. She left the restaurant that day a new person with the confidence that her Heavenly Father loved her just the way she was.

How strongholds operate

Strongholds work at the subconscious level and are not easily recognized until a major crisis in a person's life forces him or her to look deeper at the root causes of the pain. I learned that one root of the religious spirit is control. Man does not want to give up control over his life, so he creates controlled systems designed to make him feel acceptable by God. Again, this is a works-based attempt to gain God's favor, which invalidates the work of the cross. The sequence of how strongholds develop in an individual is as follows:

> Strongholds work at the subconscious level and are not easily recognized until a major crisis in a person's life forces him or her to look deeper at the root causes of the pain.

1. Satanic-inspired *thoughts* are introduced into the person's mind.
2. The individual entertains these thoughts, which bring out *emotions*.
3. Giving in to these emotions eventually leads the person to take some sort of *action*.
4. Continual participation in the action causes the individual to develop a *habit*.
5. As the habit develops, a *stronghold* is built.[7]

Imagine being born with a pair of sunglasses on. You would grow up looking at the world through those sunglasses. You would never know that you could see better without the sun-glasses unless someone revealed this to you. Now imagine tak-ing those glasses off for the first time and seeing the inside of a room much brighter and clearer. Strongholds operate this way. They masquerade as if they are part of our personality, and op-erate through us our whole life. However, the truth is that Jesus wants to totally renew our minds and hearts. Strongholds keep us from living in freedom as God meant for us to live.

I was born this way.

One of the greatest lies being propagated today in society among the gay community and the media is that people who are gay are born that way – or implying that God made them homosexual. Once we understand the truth behind this par-ticular stronghold it is easy to understand not only how those under attack have accepted this as *their truth*, but also how much of the Church has accepted this lie, as well.

> One of the greatest lies being propagated today in society among the gay com-munity and the media is that people who are gay are born that way – or implying that God made them homosexual.

Most of us hear the rationale of gay activists that they are born gay rather than their sexual preference being an influence of how they were raised and the negative exposure they had to societal factors and childhood wounds that predisposed them to this lifestyle. In February 1988, a meet-ing was held with 175 gay activists in Warrenton, Virginia. Marshall Kirk, a Harvard-educated researcher in neuropsychiatry, and Hunter Madsen, who holds a doctorate in politics from Harvard and is an expert in per-suasion tactics and social marketing, were the conveners of this meeting. They wrote a book entitled *After the Ball: How*

America Will Conquer Its Fear and Hatred of Gays in the 90's in which Kirk and Madsen made an amazing admission: "We argue that, for all practical purposes, gays should be considered to have been born gay, even though sexual orientation, for most humans, seems to be the product of a complex interaction between innate predispositions and environmental factors during childhood and early adolescence."[8]

Understanding this should not be for the purpose of putting more ammunition in our theological argument weaponry, but to assure you that those bound in this lifestyle are there because of wounds in their lives.

Gordon Dalbey, author of *Healing the Masculine Soul*, says "In praying with many men struggling against same sex attraction, my experience suggests these impulses reflect deep emotional and spiritual wounds. Most often, the boy's father has not helped him break his identification with the mother/woman by calling him out to male fellowship and identity."[9]

Danny Wallace, a friend who is a former gay in whom God delivered him from this lifestyle and now helps others caught in this lifestyle understand the origin and nature of their lifestyle. I wrote the foreword to his autobiography, *MASKquerade, A True Story of Unmasked Freedom*

> *To understand the truth surrounding anything, one must first define exactly what that thing is. Homosexuality is viewed by those in the church as simply sin. It is viewed by the secular media and the world at large as an alternative lifestyle, scripted at birth. The truth behind the mask goes far deeper.*
>
> *Homosexuality is a stronghold of the enemy, formed early in childhood to both derail the called of*

*God and distort future identity and sexuality. Homo-
sexuality never begins in the teen years or in adulthood. The root always traces back much earlier. The
deception begins during a child's defenseless, forma-
tive years — not in the womb. However, the origin is
so early in childhood that most all who struggle under
its oppression soon grow to believe that they were
"born gay."*

*Homosexuality is not about sex. It is always a
well-planned attack against the anointed of God at a
vulnerable and defenseless place in their early childhood to thwart their true destiny of greatness in the
Kingdom of God on this earth. The door he always
enters is a door that has been left wide open and un-
guarded by that male authority figure who should be
there to speak love, hope, encouragement, and a deep
affirmation that is without limit of conditions. Just as
you cannot produce one anointed Christian who will
trade the call of love to inspect another's sin, you cannot produce one homosexual male whose father loved,
adored, and treasured his heart. That person does not
exist.*

*Once the door of this stronghold is open, the seed
is planted. Once the seed is planted, the enemy is sure
to water that seed across a child's puberty development until the tree of deception has grown strong and
becomes deeply rooted. Once the leaves of sexual
manifestation appear we are confronted with a child
who is trapped and needing male affirmation inside of
an adult body that is struggling with a sexual manifestation the enemy is using to make sure true affirmation*

and love never comes, at least not from the very ones who are supposed to have the answer to their freedom. The ones who should be placing anointed hands into the dirt of this stronghold to unearth the root, are too busy picking at the leaves of manifestation that grow back as quickly as they are gathered.

To many people who are bound by the spirit of religion they declare this manifestation to be offensive and must be declared wrong. We often use the term; "Hate the sin...love the sinner," attributing the quote to Jesus. The quote was made by Gandhi. Nowhere in scripture does Jesus say that this is our call and neither did He declare it to be His mission. One takes away from the other and promotes the ridiculous situation we now face regarding the onslaught of this great stronghold. If hating the sin and loving the sinner has worked so well for us, where are all of the people who have found freedom from this great campaign of dividing love and truth? Show of hand...let's count them and rejoice! The results speak for themselves. We have produced no freedom. We have simply thrown gasoline on a great fire Satan lit, and sent religious hearts in to feverishly fan the flames.

The term gay — also meaning, and formerly commonly used to mean, happy — is part of Satan's rewriting of the language to justify the homosexual-at-birth position. To find acceptance for a situation much too horrible to face straight up, we must first redefine the language surrounding the issue. But as someone who has lived the life I can tell you that it is anything but happy.

*I know well the pain of homosexuality. I have
lived behind the mask and heard every argument
known to man surrounding the issue. Most who speak
of the issue are either seeking to find acceptance of the
lifestyle or speaking from a religious platform having little to do with redemption or healing. One is no
more wrong than the other. Satan's cruelty doesn't get
more cruel than in the deception of homosexuality,
taking hold on a person when he is too young to understand it. True freedom will come when those with
anointed hearts not only come to understand what
the enemy has done to precious lives within this - his
grandest MASKquerade of all - and reach out with the
key of our Father's great love to unlock the door and
set the captives free...one heart at at time.*

Divorce can be another entry point of dysfunctional and
wounded lives that often leads to aberrant behaviors in human
beings in each new generation. Unless there is a stopgap somewhere in the cycle, more and more expressions of aberrant behavior will be the result until we end up like the Roman Empire
and disintegrate from within.

If we had a 3% divorce rate in America instead of being
more than 50% we would not be fighting issues around gay rights
because there would be far less innocent children attacked by
this stronghold. However, simply staying in the marriage is not
enough. We men must stand guard in the Father's rich love and
affirmation over our children. The Church is now fighting the
wrong battle. Healthy marriages must be our focus. That is the
only solution to this issue. People who are caught in the homosexual stronghold are children who have been wounded somewhere

in their past who are crying out for love and acceptance. The more they feel rejected by society, the more radical they become. Only the love of Jesus Christ can heal marriages and individuals. A spirit of rejection always cries out for acceptance.

A few years ago there was a documentary released about a young boy who was seen playing with girls toys and obviously having effeminate tendencies exhibited in his life. Gay activists jumped on the bandwagon around this video proclaiming, "See, he was born that way." The implication was that he was made that way by God. That is a false conclusion. He may have certainly been born that way, but the reason he was exhibiting such behavior could be traced back to generational iniquity.

> If we had a 3% divorce rate in America instead of being more than 50% we would not be fighting issues around gay rights

My good friend Craig Hill shared a story in his book, The Power of a Parent's Blessing, which demonstrates how this can happen in a child. I highly recommend his book if you want to see how the power of a parent's blessing can effect the life of a child.

Freedom for Susan's Son

At an Ancient Paths Experience I was conducting several years ago, Susan came up to me at a break with great concern for her five-year-old son, Billy. Billy was absolutely consumed with sexual lust in a very abnormal way, his mother reported. His mouth was continually spouting sexual obscenities. He knew all the latest sexual jokes. He voraciously devoured any type of pornography he could find.

"Worst of all," expressed the distraught mother, "one day a couple of weeks ago I left Billy alone in a room with his little one-and-a-half-year-old baby sister. I couldn't

*have been gone for more than three minutes, and when I
returned, I found Billy unclothed and attempting to enter
into sexual relationship with his baby sister. It scared me
to death," Susan said.*

"*This is not normal for a five-year-old even to be aware
of such things," cried Susan. "I don't know where he
could have picked up this type of thinking and behavior.
He has never, to our knowledge, been around people who
think or act this way. My husband and I are very careful
about what kind of friends Billy plays with. He has never
been sexually molested. Of course, now no other parents
will let their children play with Billy. We just don't know
what to do. He is a constant embarrassment to me. I can't
take him anywhere, because I never know what he is going
to do or say. I have to watch him continually at home for
fear of his molesting the baby. We've tried praying for him,
taking him to a psychiatrist, and everything we know of;
but nothing seems to help.*"

*Susan's pastor was sitting with me as she described her
son's behavior. Her pastor confirmed that it was indeed
as bad as she depicted, and that they had done everything
they knew to do. I didn't have any answers for them, so
I suggested that we pray. As we became quiet before the
Lord, I felt the Lord lead me to begin to ask Susan a series
of questions.*

"*Let's just start at the very beginning of Billy's life," I
said. "Can you tell me, how was your son conceived?*"

*Susan sat in silence for several seconds, as tears began
to stream down her cheeks. Then she began, "I was not
walking with God at that time in my life. As a matter of
fact, I was living a very lust-filled and immoral lifestyle.*

As close as I can tell, the night that Billy was conceived, I was with several different men. I wouldn't even have any idea which one might have been his father. This lifestyle continued for another three months or so, and then I gave my life to the Lord Jesus. Since that time I have been walking with the Lord and have had no more involvement in sexual immorality. Shortly after Billy was born, I met my husband, who is a godly man. We married and have been serving the Lord ever since."

As Susan shared this information, the Lord brought to my mind a very strange thought. Perhaps little Billy had actually been demonized by a spirit of sexual lust right at the time of conception. His current behavior could be a result of the influence of that demonic spirit in his life. I had never previously thought of this possibility. However, I felt very strongly that I should mention it to the pastor and to Susan. As I shared this thought, Susan began to weep profusely, now feeling extremely guilty.

"I'm sure that is probably exactly what happened," she exclaimed through her tears.

"Is your son here with you? I asked

"No, he is at home with his father," replied Susan. "What should we do? I have already repented of the sexual immorality of the past. But how can we get Billy free of the spirit of lust?"

I then explained to Susan and also to the pastor the Strong Man principle and that when a child is conceived outside of the spiritually protective hedge of marriage, there is nothing to protect a child from the demonic world. The covenant of marriage is that protective hedge that blocks demonic access to children in the womb. Neither *the pastor, nor Susan had ever realized this before.*

Explaining to Susan that she was the strong man, and in the area of her bondage to lust, she had opened the door in her son's life to a demonic spirit to afflict him in the same area. Usually good news is made only relevant by understanding the true impact of the bad news. I then went on to explain to Susan that while she had authority as a mother to open the door, she also had authority to close the same spiritual door and to then command the demonic spirit to leave her son with the authority she now had as a believer in Jesus Christ.

I then asked the pastor if he had any experience with deliverance from demonic spirits. He answered affirmatively that he had. I then instructed Susan that she and her husband should bring their son to their pastor's office and take the following steps together.

1. *Personally renounce the iniquities of fornication, sexual immorality and lust in her own life.*
2. *Pray to close the door to the life of her son, which she had opened through her own bondage to lust.*
3. *Dispatch the iniquity of lust to the cross of Jesus Christ, Who died to take upon Himself all of our transgressions and iniquities (Isaiah 53:4-6).*
4. *Pray to break the power of that iniquity over the life of the five-year-old son.*
5. *Pray to exchange the iniquity of lust in the life of the son for the blessing of sexual and emotional purity that Jesus died to pay for.*
6. *Exercise her authority in Christ and as a strong man (parent) to command the demonic spirit of lust to*

leave her son immediately and go to the place where Jesus Christ sends it.

7. *Ask the Holy Spirit to fill her son with Himself.*

Susan and her pastor agreed to have this meeting with the family the following week. Several months later I returned to that same city again speaking in another conference. Immediately following my conference session, Susan came running excitedly up to me, with a little boy in tow.

"Remember me, remember me?" she excitedly exclaimed.

I actually didn't remember her by sight, as I had spoken at many meetings since that time. She then began to explain her situation to me, and I immediately remembered.

"We did what you said," she exclaimed. "My husband and I met with our pastor and our son. We followed the steps you outlined, and when we got to the step to command the spirit of lust to leave our son, we saw a visible manifestation of it leaving and a total change of our son's countenance."

Susan then burst into tears, picked up her little boy in her arms and proclaimed, "I got my son back; I got my son back! He is a normal little five-year-old boy, who doesn't know anything about sex. He is totally innocent and doesn't remember any of the sexual jokes or even understand anything about it. He is not alive to sex at all. When we commanded that spirit to leave him, it did, and there was an instant transformation in my son as from darkness to light. His countenance instantly changed, as did his language and behavior. Thank you so much."

Susan was almost beside herself with joy and just couldn't stop thanking the Lord for setting her son free.

"I never before would have believed that it was possible for a little boy to be demonized at the moment of conception had it not happened to my son, and had I not seen the consequences of my bondage to the iniquity of lust with my own eyes," exclaimed Susan.

Parents are Gatekeepers for their Children

The experience I had with Susan and her son dramatically demonstrated to me the serious charge that parents have from the Lord as gatekeepers, or strong men in the lives of their children. Since that time, I have encountered many similar situations in several other families. When the covenant of marriage is not in place and a child is conceived, that child is potentially subject to demonic influence. Once I understood this, I was able to understand why some people bound in a lifestyle of homosexuality told me that they were absolutely convinced they were born with such feelings and identity.

As a believer, I had always thought that they could not have been born with a homosexual identity, but must have acquired such sometime in childhood. However, in ministering to one such young man, I had asked him how long his homosexual identity had been with him. He responded that he was quite certain it was from birth. As we prayed, I heard the Lord tell me that he was indeed born with that identity, but that he was not created that way. Because his parents were not married and had provided him no spiritual hedge of protection in conception and while in the womb, this young man had been demonized by a sexually perverse spirit while yet in the womb. So when he said that he was born that way, he was indeed correct. After understanding the origin of his homosexual identity, we were then able to minister to him, and help him obtain deliverance and freedom. Since that time, I have seen this same scenario many times in the lives of various people, and have come to understand the critical importance of being blessed at the time of conception with the spiritual hedge of protection provided by the covenant of marriage.[11]

In a 1998 interview with Rick Knoth, managing editor of the Assemblies of God *Enrichment Journal*, Promise Keepers founder and president, Bill McCartney stated, that they had researched and found that 62% of Christian men admitted to struggles with sexual sin--pornography, adultery, and sensuality. How could this be? When Christians value the Father more for what He can do for them than for intimacy and love, they eventually begin to seek to fulfill their own selfish desires rather than enjoy the relationship they have with God. Then, in order to fill the void that has been created, they seek comfort or identity in one or more of the counterfeit

> 62% of Christian men admitted to struggles with sexual sin--pornography, adultery, and sensuality.

affections--power, possessions, position, people, places, performance, or passions of the flesh. This vicious cycle can continue until they realize that what they are lusting for will not satisfy them and that they have unmet needs for love and intimacy that only Father God's embrace can fulfill. [12]

Renouncing Spiritual Strongholds

Many of us may have been impacted by generational iniquity from our family lines. The result may be that we struggle with spiritual strongholds. But God does not want us to continue to be ruled by them or to impose them upon anyone else. If you recognize that you are operating under the influence of a stronghold, renounce it in prayer, repent for what you've done, ask God's forgiveness and the forgiveness of others, and resist the return of the spirit or stronghold. Receive God's power to forsake it, and ask Him to make you sensitive to the times when you are tempted to act in a wrong spirit. Move into freedom by asking God to fill you afresh with the power of His Holy Spirit.

When you encounter a person who is influenced by a stronghold, let your first response be prayer. Ask God for wisdom and love and for Him to set the person free. If the person has offended you, forgive him or her and don't let that person's actions or attitudes keep a grip on you. Picture him in a prison that you have the keys to open through prayer. Live your life based on a genuine faith rooted in Jesus' life and example.

Most of all, continually become transformed by the renewing of your mind, as we are told to do in Romans 12:2. This is your best insurance against any spiritual influences that do not come from God. As you develop a strong relationship with God through the power of His Spirit, not only will you become empowered to bring the Kingdom to those around you at work, but also you will be able to resist Satan's sabotage.

Prayer of Repentance to Renounce Strongholds

We must gain freedom by renouncing and repenting of the influence of strongholds. Once you identify strongholds in your life, please pray this prayer. Use the self-assessment worksheet on the next page to identify strongholds in your life. If married, I recommend you both take it individually and separately on behalf of the other and combine the results.

Prayer for Deliverance from Strongholds

Father in heaven, I come before you in the Name of Jesus. I recognize the power You have given me by the shed blood of

Jesus to demolish spiritual strongholds in my life. I confess that I have given a foothold to the sin(s) of _____ *(list them)* _____. *I renounce the stronghold of* _____ *by the authority of the Name of Jesus Christ according to Your Word.*

I take back through Your power that ground that I surrendered to the enemy. I pray that You will fill me with trust and grounded obedience to Your Holy Spirit so that this area of my life will be in conformity to the image of Christ. Amen.

For more detail information on this topic we suggest you visit www.tgifbookstore.com and order *Demolishing Strongholds workbook* by Mike and Sue Dowgewicz and *Broken Children, Grown Up Pain* by Dr. Paul Hegstrom.

Use the self-assessment worksheet on the next page to identify strongholds in your life. If married, I recommend you both take it individually and separate on behalf of the other and combine the results.

Questions for Reflection and Discussion

1. Explain the difference between generation iniquity and a stronghold.

2. What is the root of homosexuality? Why are failure in marriage and a father wound the leading causes of homosexuality?

3. Why does the Church make homosexuality the unpardonable sin when it has a divorce rate greater than non-believers? What must change if we are to see this growing trend toward homosexuality decrease?

Strongholds and Their Symptoms

Deceit—Total ____
____ Lying
____ Fantasies
____ Delusions
____ Rationalization
____ Wrong doctrine/
     Misuse of
     scripture

*Confusion (Doubt
& Unbelief)*—____
____ Suspicious
____ Apprehensive
____ Indecisive
____ Skeptical
____ Unsettled

*Independence
& Divorce*—____
____ Insensitive
____ Lonely/Aloof
____ Self-determined
____ Withdrawn
____ Excuse making
____ Lack of trust
____ "Martyr" complex

Control—____
____ Manipulative
____ Striving
____ Lacking trust
____ Insensitive
____ Desiring
     recognition
____ Violent

*Stupor &
Prayerlessness*—____
____ Distanced from
     God – cold love
____ Distracted
____ Spiritual blindness
____ Laziness
____ Deceived self-
     appraisal

Pride—____
____ Vain
____ Self-righteous
____ Self-centered
____ Insensitive
____ Insensitive
____ Materialistic
____ Seeks positions

Bitterness—____
____ Resentment
____ Racism
____ Unforgiveness
____ Anger/Hatred
____ Violence
____ Revenge

Rejection—____
____ Addictive behavior
____ Compulsions
____ Seeks acceptance
____ Unworthiness
____ Withdrawal

Sexual Impurity—____
____ Lust
____ Seductiveness
____ Masturbation
____ Fornication
____ Adultery
____ Frigidity
____ Homosexuality
____ Pornography

Rebellion—____
____ Self-willed
____ Stubborn
____ Pouting
____ Strife
____ Factious
____ Divisive
____ Anger leads to
     argument
____ Independent
____ Unteachable

Heaviness—____
____ Depression
____ Despair
____ Self-pity
____ Loneliness
____ Unconfessed sin
____ Suicidal thoughts

Strongholds and Their Symptoms (continued)

Idolatry—____

____ Frustrated

____ Hopeless

____ Greedy/selfish

____ Financial problems

____ Wrong goals/ decisions

____ Living a lie

____ Apathetic

Jealousy—____

____ Spiteful

____ Gossip/slander

____ Betrayal

____ Critical nature

____ Judgmental

____ Suspicious

Religiosity—____

____ Seeks activities

____ No spiritual power

____ Spiritual blindness

____ Hypocritical

Fear & Insecurity—____

____ Inferiority

____ Inadequacy

____ Timidity

____ Pleasing people, not God

____ Lack of trust/ worry

____ Phobias

____ Perfectionism

____ Dread of failure

____ Inability to set goals

____ "Motor-mouth"

Sample

Deceit—Total _5_

_6_ Lying

_2_ Fantasies

_1_ Delusions

_9_ Rationalization

_7_ Wrong doctrine/ Misuse of scripture

Total the number of symptoms under each heading.

Ex: 6+2+1+9+7 = 25

Divide by the number of symptoms in that category.

Ex: 25 :–5 = 5

5 is the total for the "Deceit" category.

Suggested Prayer

In the name and authority of the Lord Jesus Christ, I renounce the influence of

_____

_____

_____

in Jesus' name and by His shed blood on the cross in order that I can be free to know and choose to do the will of God. As children of God seated with Christ in the heavenlies, we agree that every enemy of the Lord Jesus Christ be bound. In Jesus' name. Amen.

Source: *Demolishing Strongholds workbook*, Mike and Sue Dowgiewicz, Aslan Group Publishing ©1996

How long, O you sons of men,
will you turn my glory to shame?
How long will you love worthlessness
and seek falsehood?
—Psalm 4:2

Overcoming Childhood Wounds and the False Self

Bruce Willis starred in a movie in the year 2000 entitled *The Kid*. Russell was a 40 year old single, egocentric executive that ran an image consulting business for high profile politicians, business executives and TV anchors. His rude, abrupt, over confident, narcissistic "the world revolves around me", attitude was the personality he hid behind. Life had to revolve around him and when others got in the way, he dismissed them. He had no patience for weak people who did things with anything less than excellence. He had the best of everything—cars, home, girlfriend, clothes, etc. Whatever he wanted he bought. He moved from one client to another, solved their image problems, something he took great efforts to maintain for himself. In essence, his job was to polish the false-self (poser) image of each of his clients in order to give them the image they feel their public wanted to see and wanted to maintain.

Russell was a person filled with bitterness toward his father and refused to have any relationship with him. The root of his bitterness went back to when he was eight years old.

One day an eight year old chubby kid showed up in his ultra-modern bachelor pad. He discovered that this wasn't just any little boy—he was Russell himself incarnated at the age of eight. Through the rest of the movie Russell rediscovered his childhood through Rusty (his eight year old version of himself). Rusty began to inquire about the adult version of himself and he concluded that he grew up to be a failure because none of his childhood dreams came true. He wasn't married, didn't have a dog and did not fly airplanes for a living—everything he dreamt he would grow up to fulfill which would equate to success in his mind. He challenged Russell to find out what went wrong. Together they go on a journey of discovery to revisit some key events that made Russell the man he became.

Russell had a girlfriend who partly put up with his selfish and egocentric ways because she saw something in him she actually liked. However, his negative, independent and protective personality all but drove her away until she discovered the young Rusty and fell in love with the personable young boy and began to wonder what happened that produced the adult Russell. Together Russell and Rusty began to piece their childhood memories together and actually relived them to discover how Russell became so dysfunctional in his personality.

One day Rusty turned to his older self (Russell) and said, "I get what you do now. You help people lie about who they really are so they can pretend to be someone else who they are not." "Yeah, kid. I guess you are right," responded Russell. The truth of his life began to unfold.

The climax of the story unfolds when little Rusty replayed a scene with his father outside his home when his terminally diagnosed mother had to go pick him up from school for fighting. His father was extremely upset with Rusty for making his mother go to the school to pick him up.

"You're killing your mother! How could you make your mother have to come get you!?" he screamed to his face as he shook him with both hands. Little Rusty was devastated. It was a life-defining moment for Rusty. His life would never be the same. *This became an agreement over his life that he would live out as an adult.* "I am flawed. I killed my mother. I'm shameful." He would spend a lifetime trying to cover-up his shame to become someone others would accept and respect. The bitterness he held toward his father would remain throughout his adult years.

As he grew older his false-self became a hard shell that he hid behind designed to protect him from anyone who might hurt him again since his own parents did not protect him. His egocentric executive personality became his outer protective shell personality. As Russell began to recognize the truth of his situation, he began to change his behavior and ultimately became a new person by the end of the movie. He realized his father was reacting out of his own pain and forgave his father after holding onto years of bitterness. He began to reveal his true personality that was actually caring and sensitive. His heart was being healed to become the man he was created to be. By the end of the movie we see him in the future--making a career change to become a pilot and even had a dog. He married his girlfriend.

I so identified with Russell's character in the movie. When I began my own ad agency in the early 80's I was driven to succeed like Russell. Although I was a Christian, I often found myself conflicted between the need to succeed and the desire to be led by God and be sensitive to His direction. Traits of stubbornness, selfishness, independence and ego would show up. I struggled with this side of me, wrestling with what Paul describes in Romans when he says "there is something inside of me that does what I do not want to do. It is the sin within me." I may not have exhibited the same level of dysfunction Russell displayed, but I did struggle inside, keeping it in check as a good Christian should. The biggest problem was that it operated at a subconscious level.

The false-self of competence and performance was seeking to deal with the unknown, unrecognized pain that drove me to my subconscious need to be validated through my performance and success. The problem was it was mixed with a genuine relationship with God that helped soften the false-self but never allowed me to see the outer core for what it was—a protection against being hurt that was a result of childhood wounds. It represented a conflict between God's glory in me and that which sought to mask my true self. The false-self is rooted in shame and falsehood.

Competence becomes our method of dealing with a wounded heart

When I was a child, I spoke as a child, I understood as a child, I thought as a child; but when I became a man, I put away childish things. For now we see in a mirror, dimly, but then face to face. Now I know in part, but then I shall know just as I also am known. —1 Corinthians 13:11-12

Arrested Development

Although Russell was a financially successful man, he acted like an emotional 8 year old as an adult that required the world to revolve around him. Arrested development is a term that describes how adults revert back to an emotional state of their childhood. They are in essence "arrested" at that age and never mature past that age emotionally as an adult. They may at one moment act like an adult but the next

> Arrested development that is caused by the wounds of childhood amplifies or magnifies our sin nature

minute revert to childish behavior because they have been frozen within two years of the age of their woundedness. Dr. Paul Hegstrom, author of Broken Children, Grown Up Pain, explains that "arrested development that is caused by the wounds of childhood amplifies or magnifies our sin nature. The deeper the wounds, the more we act selfishly and childishly. When we have too much childhood trauma, we are hindered in our ability to develop genuine healthy relationships with our Creator and others close to us. We can't readily reach out or accept others—because our wounds have made us unteachable, unable to trust and afraid of truth. We can't embrace grace and mercy, so we struggle with accepting what's freely given."[13]

Arrested development sabotages the heart's good intentions and turns us into a spiritual hypocrite

I discovered that shame, performance and the death of my dad at age 14 all contributed to arrested development in my own life. In order to mature emotionally, it required revisiting, just like Russell did, the events of the wounds. Gaining healing from those wounds was required to move into emotional maturity.

Pop star Michael Jackson died suddenly in July 2009 from a prescription drug overdose. Jackson is one of the most extreme cases of arrested development you will ever witness. It was widely known that Jackson was physically abused as a child by his father. Jackson's father often held the kids upside down, tripping them, pushing them into walls, screaming, shouting, and frightening them. Michael shared that he often cried from loneliness and sometimes got sick or started to vomit upon seeing his father.

> As we learn the truth about our past we can begin to walk in the truth of who God made us to be

He recalled his dad sitting in a chair with a belt in his hand when he and his siblings rehearsed and hearing his dad say, "If you don't do it the right way, I will tear you up." These were early childhood wounds that caused arrested development in Michael.

The world watched this grown man live as a child emotionally. He even built a multi-acre theme park home called NeverLand, complete with amusement rides. He loved spending time with kids, but did not relate to them as an adult, but actually as a fellow child. People who knew him often referred to him as childlike. Jackson was probably arrested in development around the age of 9 emotionally.

"And you shall know the truth, and the truth shall make you free". —John 8:32

Dr. Hegstrom cites that "most of the time, just the knowing that our behaviors have a source will restart the growing process. Denial blocks the growing process. The mind needs to understand that there's a reason, not an excuse." As we learn the truth about our past we can begin to walk in the truth of who God made us to be. Knowing the truth about your past becomes the first step toward freedom and healing.

Let me encourage you to revisit your childhood. Were there any events that traumatized you? Do you struggle with certain sins as an adult? Ask God to reveal the time this may have caused arrested development in your life. Ask God to heal those places of hurt. Begin to walk in the healing and freedom God has for you.

Questions for Reflection and Discussion

1. What was the "agreement" Russell made with himself when he was a child?

2. Explain "arrested development" and its affect on us as adults.

3. Why is learning the truth about our past important to gaining freedom?

There is a way that seems right to a man,
but its end is the way of death.
—*Proverbs 16:25*

Overcoming
the False-self — Poser

he movie, Groundhog Day, is a classic comedy made in 1993 starring Bill Murray and Andie MacDowell. Murray plays an ambitious, weatherman for a Pittsburgh TV station. He is egocentric, prideful, narcissistic, selfish, brash, opinionated, rude and driven to get out of his perceived lowlife dead-end job. He wants a bigger market job, but until then he performs his duties with sarcasm and intolerance with his co-workers, one of which is an attractive producer (MacDowell) he treats with contempt.

Legend has it that the groundhog will determine whether there will be six months of more cold weather, or an early spring. It has become a ritual that the town is known for. Phil's assignment is to cover the annual Groundhog Day celebration located in the small, rural town of Punxsutawney, Pennsylvania that is filled with down home local people that Phil has little tolerance for in his assignment because he is too important for them and should not even have to cover such an event with his talent.

The story finds Phil going through his day with an abhorrent attitude toward every person he meets along the way. He snaps at his producer and cameraman as they prepare to do the live broadcast. He makes sarcastic remarks just before airtime. However, on camera, he is the ultimate professional "poser" commentator and delivers just what the audience wants to hear. It is a contrast in personalities—his on camera personality and his real personality.

Phil is living his life in a false self, or poser. It is a personality that has been developed from childhood designed to protect

The false-self is born out of a wound to our heart

him from what happened in his early childhood years. It presents to others the person he feels others will accept. It is a mask to prevent him from connecting to a wound that shut down his heart and true self early in life.

A snow storm moves into the area that forces him to stay overnight. He awakens at 6 AM to discover he is reliving the same day as before. After getting past the initial shock and unbelief, he goes throughout the day encountering the same people, conversations, and events he encountered the previous day.

Throughout the movie Phil discovers the condition of his heart with each new day that he lives, over and over and over. Gradually he discovers that when he begins to change his response to each irritating event in his day to a more sensitive and caring response, he notices the people relate to him in a more loving and caring way. He begins to connect with others at a heart level and learns that his brash behavior does not get the desired outcome that he wants, so he begins to change. He discovers that when he begins to connect with others at a heart level by being considerate and kind, he discovers he likes this

version of Phil. He realizes there is something good, even fulfilling to this new personality. Because he relives the same day so
many times, he begins to change his response to each encounter
with people throughout the day, which ultimately endears the
town-folk to embrace him as a loving and caring person.

He becomes the favorite son in the town. He finds his female producer very attractive but she hates his first day egocentric personality. However, she is now being drawn to his
new, caring nature that is now being exhibited toward her and
others.

Once the transformation is complete, he awakens one
morning to find his producer friend lying next to him on the
bed and he realizes his "nightmare" is over and that he has won
the heart of his producer, and the entire town.

The false-self is born out of a wound to our heart. It protects us from others being able to see our true heart. It operates
on a subconscious level. We find a few gifts and abilities that
we do well and they become the impenetrable wall that we hide
our true heart behind. Our heart actually gets shut down when
we are operating from a place of performance, independence
and superficial relationships. Consequently, our mates view us
relationally as cold and distant.

"I was afraid because I was naked; so I hid."
—*Genesis 3:10*

Whenever we are wounded we seek to hide from our true
self because our shame says we will not be acceptable to others
as we are. We are driven to hide behind our fig leaf (false-self)
that protects us from our true self. This all happens on a subconscious basis as a built-in protection mechanism from wounds we

received as a child. Earlier we cited that the story of your life is the story of the long and destructive assault on your heart by Satan who knows what you could become and fears it. Satan wants your true heart to remain hidden behind your wounds.

The marketplace encourages us to live behind our fig leaf in order to succeed at all costs.

There is a passage in Isaiah 50 described in the Amplified Bible that expresses this issue better than any scripture I know: "Who is among you who [reverently] fears the Lord, who obeys the voice of His Servant, yet who walks in darkness and deep trouble and has no shining splendor [in his heart]? Let him rely on, trust in, and be confident in the name of the Lord, and let him lean upon and be supported by his God. Behold, all you [enemies of your own selves] who attempt to kindle your own fires [and work out your own plans of salvation], who surround and gird yourselves with momentary sparks, darts, and firebrands that you set aflame! — walk by the light of your self-made fire and of the sparks that you have kindled [for yourself, if you will]! But this shall you have from My hand: you shall lie down in grief and in torment" (Isaiah 50:10-11).

The false-self is a self-made fire that prevents us from seeing our own splendor in our heart. It masquerades a false heart that only causes internal torment.

King Saul's False Self

King Saul lived behind a false-self, poser image. He thought of himself as a spiritual leader. However, underneath that false-self, poser, lay an insecure man who needed the praise of man to validate him as a man and a leader. Gene Edwards helps us understand the subtle trap that is often laid for those who never connect with their true heart.

Many men pray for the power of God. More every year. Those prayers sound powerful, sincere, godly and without ulterior motive. Hidden under such prayer and fervor, however, are ambition, a craving for fame, the desire to be considered a spiritual giant. The man who prays such prayer may not even know it, but such dark motives and desires are in his heart...in your heart.

Even as men pray these prayers, they are hollow inside. There is little internal spiritual growth. Prayer for power is the quick and the short way, circumnavigating internal growth.

There is a vast difference between the outward clothing of the Spirit's power and the inward filling of the Spirit's life. In the first, despite the power, the hidden man of the heart may remain unchanged. In the latter, that monster is dealt with.[14]

Pharisees were the ultimate posers. We, too, can be posers when we play roles that are imposters of our true self instead of living from our true heart. Jesus rebuked what He saw as superficial faith and a life that was not lived from the heart.

The enemy of our souls tries to convince us that in order to survive we must hide behind our false self that is the safe place from which we can operate. We settle for a smaller story of our lives when we live from this place. God desires us to live from our true self "in the inward parts" (Psalm 51:6) and when we do this "He will teach us wisdom in the inmost place." Satan tries to steal our glory by convincing us to live a lie. "How long, O you sons of men, will you turn my glory to shame? How long will you love worthlessness and seek falsehood?" (Psalm 4:2).

I realized that I was beginning to use my God-given gifts as a teacher, speaker and strategic Christian leader to gain people's admiration and praise. This is a subtle trap of the enemy. The more we are defined by performance, the more we are susceptible to this scheme. God does not desire us to get our validation from those we are called to serve. We are to get our validation from Him alone. We are to play to an audience of ONE.

> The enemy of our souls tries to convince us that in order to survive we must hide behind our false self that is the safe place from which we can operate

George MacDonald wrote, "As soon as [any] service is done for the honor and not for the service-sake, the doer is that moment outside the Kingdom." Competency is the idol of the marketplace believer that shields us from our true self and intimacy with God and others. Oswald Chambers said, "Beware of posing as a profound person— God became a baby."

Consider areas where you are not living from your true self. Why not stop living a life you think others will accept. Live from your heart alone.

Questions for Reflection and Discussion

1. In the movie Groundhog Day, the character Phil was an example of a poser. Explain the concept of living as a "poser".

2. What is the root of independence, pride and self-protection?

3. What does it look like to live from your true self?

I will give you a new heart and put a new spirit within you; I will take the heart of stone out of your flesh and give you a heart of flesh. I will put My Spirit within you and cause you to walk in My statutes, and you will keep My judgments and do them.
—*Ezekiel 36:26-28*

Overcoming by Discovering Your True Self

On different occasions a close friend used to say to me, "Excuse me, who are you talking to?" Her inference was that my countenance and language had changed from talking from my heart to speaking to her as if I was teaching a seminar. I was oblivious to this trait. My daughter had made similar statements. The false-self poser is something that is ingrained in us and we flow into it naturally unless those close to us know and recognize it and can help us get free of it. We need to invite this input if we are serious about change.

Dr. Paul Hegstrom, founder and president of Life Skills International and author of *Broken Children, Grown Up Pain* calls the false self a pseudo personality. "For the wounded person, the mask never really goes away. We protect ourselves by showing different personalities when we're with different people. We create our pseudo personality to meet the expectations of important people in our lives—we're certain they'll reject us if they see our defective-ness. If our coworkers don't see the real or core us, it's harder for us to be hurt by them. The mask protects our vulnerability. Self-preservation is the reason it's possible for workaholic and apathetic employees to mask their wounds. The workaholic is performance-oriented and connects his or her worth with how much he or she

> Research reveals that within six to seven months after taking a new job, our core personality will become dominant, but rarely before then

can accomplish. 'Staying alive and being valuable means I must keep doing and achieving,' thinks the workaholic." Dr. Hegstrom also found that his research reveals that within six to seven months after taking a new job, our core person-ality will become dominant, but rarely before then. The negative traits exempli-fied by operation of a pseudo personality then begin to surface.[15]

Dr. Hegstrom helped me see that performance has played a key role in my own early development and it has affected my relationships and ministry. There were times when I sensed the presence of God in my activities, but other times I was clearly operating from a performance-based motivation and looking for validation of my work from others instead of God.

John Eldredge, in his book *Wild at Heart*, provides the fol-lowing insights on how we prop ourselves up through various things we do or want to be known by.

The world offers a man a false sense of power and a false sense of security. Be brutally honest now—where does your own sense of power come from? Is it how pretty your wife is—or your secretary? Is it how many people attend your church? Is it knowledge—that you have an expertise and that makes others come to

you, bow to you? Is it your position, degree, or title?
A white coat, a PH.D., a podium, or a paneled office
can make a man feel like pretty neat stuff. What hap-
pens inside you when I suggest you give it up? Put the
book down for a few moments and consider what you
would think of yourself if tomorrow you lost every-
thing that the world has rewarded you for.[16]

"Without Christ, a man must fail miserably" says
{George} MacDonald, "or succeed even more miser-
ably." Jesus warns us against anything that gives us a
false sense of power.[17]

Anything that props us up and makes us feel better about
ourselves is a false self, or poser. It could be our accomplishments in sports, career achievements, our ability to win the
hearts of women, being seen and affirmed as a great Christian
leader, having great charisma or attractive-
ness—all of these become our "drugs" of
choice to maintain our false self designed
to protect us from our true self. God allows some of these traits, which are actually God-given, to be destroyed in order
to connect us with the wound that these are seeking to hide.

> Anything that props us up and makes us feel better about ourselves is a false self, or poser

Recently I have gone through a season where everything I
could possibly receive validation from was removed from me
for a period of time. Some of these things I removed myself,
others were removed without my say in the matter. In essence
there was a removal of anything I could control or gain validation from. Some of these actions were a result of my own stubbornness in not being able to see truth due to my childhood
woundedness that set up boundaries of defense against truth.

I can tell you that when all of these things are removed from your life, there is a shock to your system. We cannot survive unless Christ alone is our all and even then we face an enormous loss of value, sense of belonging and feelings of abandonment.

God allows us to recognize and revisit our wounds in order to be healed and to live from our true self. Unfortunately, most men refuse to recognize or acknowledge their wound because of fear and pride. Our false self is often strengthened even more when we feel threatened. Sometimes it takes a total crash before some men are willing to examine the root of their problems.

> The false self must ultimately die if we are to ever have intimacy in our lives with God and others

Validation of our lives cannot come through our spouses or close relationships, our careers or others we may seek to impress. Validation can only come from God. When there are unresolved wounds, we cling to our natural gifts that God wants to put a sword through in order to reveal His life through them. Once we recognize our false-self masks, we must voluntarily begin to dismantle them in order to reveal our true self.

The false self prevents us from having intimacy with God and others in our lives. God's love of his sons and daughters drives Him to destroy the false self in us in order for true intimacy to be realized by each of us.

The false self must ultimately die if we are to ever have intimacy in our lives with God and others. Jesus said in Luke 9:24: "Whoever wants to save his life will lose it." Deep down inside we are all seeking to be loved by God and others in our lives. However, because of our wounds we build a wall around our hearts through our competencies. One of my early wounds was the death of my father from an airplane crash at age 14 and subsequent decline in our financial standard of living because the insurance did not pay off. This left our family in a difficult place and my mom often said, "We don't have enough money for that." A life message was born and I lived it out by seeking to insulate myself from that ever happening to me as an adult. I became a workaholic, driven to success and independence. This led to seeking love through validation of others and performance. It was a superficial love that provided the fuel for the false self. God destroyed that false self by attacking these strengths through a marriage crisis.

One of the only ways to heal our hearts is to discover the Father's love for us. David Benner, author of *Surrender to Love*, describes his own journey out of the false self to experiencing the Father's love:

> *Daring to accept myself and receive love for who I am in my nakedness and vulnerability is the indispensable precondition for genuine transformation. But make no mistake about just how difficult this is. Everything within me wants to show my best "pretend self" to both other people and God. This is my false self—the self of my own making. This self can never be transformed, because it is never willing to receive love in vulnerability. When this pretend self receives love, it simply becomes stronger and I am even more deeply in bondage to my false ways of living. Both popular psychology and spirituality—even popular Christian spirituality—tend to reinforce this false self by playing to our deep-seated belief in self-improvement. Both also play to our instinctual tendency to attempt to get our act together by ourselves before we receive love.*

The life and message of Jesus stand diametrically op-
posed to such effort at self-improvement. Jesus did not
come to encourage our self-transformation schemes.
He understood that rather than longing to receive his
love in an undefended state, what we really want is to
manipulate God to accept us in our false and defended
ways of being. If only He would remain unaware of
just how desperately we need real love.

How tarrying it is to face my naked and needy
self—the self that longs for love and knows it can do
nothing to manipulate the universe into providing the
only kind of love I really need. The crux of the prob-
lem is that I cannot feel the love of God because I do
not dare to accept it unconditionally. To know that I
am loved, I must accept the frightening helplessness
and vulnerability that is my true state. This is always
terrifying.[18]

Our talents and abilities are God-given. It is when we hide behind them that we fall prey to the false self. God desires to reveal His glory through these gifts through an intimate relationship with us.

The wound is designed to destroy us. Satan attacks us in the place of our inheritance. For Moses, Satan tried to kill him at birth and then shut his mouth up through a stuttering spirit. For Jacob, Satan tried to deceive him into thinking he had to deceive and manipulate others to gain what he needed in life. This is what he did to his brother Esau.

God brought Moses to the place of his wound when He challenged him to speak for Him to the Egyptian Pharaoh. He challenged him and made him confront his early wound. For

Jacob, it was in his relationships. His false self was manifested through control and manipulation of others to protect him. God had to take him into the place of his wound through his uncle Laban. He was able to see himself through his controlling uncle. When Jacob wrestled with the angel, God healed something in Jacob that was significant enough that God would recognize the event by changing his name from Jacob to Israel, "one who wrestles with God."

For me, Satan tried to shut down my emotions, speech and writing through childhood wounds given through my parents. They did not do these things intentionally; they were simply passing on what they learned from their parents. God brought me face to face with my wounds through a marriage crisis that led to a divorce.

> The ultimate goal is intimacy with our Heavenly Father and others in our lives

Once God took me to the place of woundedness and I began to understand the truth, I began to be healed and become free from the false self. I am still a work in progress. Most men don't want to face pain. We desensitize our hearts through the things we do that cover our deep wounds that reside in us all. To find our core self we must recognize how we cover up our pain through the false self, or poser. This blocks intimacy with God and others.

Once we recognize and revisit the pain and get healed, we will begin to fulfill the glory of the life purpose God intends for each of us to experience. For me, it is in writing and speaking and living in intimate relationship with my Heavenly Father and others. Up until then, I sought to accomplish these through my natural strengths and performance.

The ultimate goal is intimacy with our Heavenly Father and others in our lives. All of the life stories of key characters in the scriptures reveal their journey toward intimacy with God the Father. Many of these individuals had to come out of their own dysfunctional family systems to gain healing for their earlier wounds in order to mature into God's purposes for their lives. Consider Abraham, Jacob, and David to name a few.

Lessons from David

Early in the life of David we see something different in his life. His life was born out of relationship. Even as a teen shepherd he experienced times of solitude, worship and work. He honed his skills in the fields as a shepherd, killing the lion and the bear. He honed his relationship with God through solitude and worship. No one saw him do these things. They were done from a desire deep within his heart. His performance was to an audience of One and maybe a few sheep. This integration of faith, worship, work and solitude went with him his whole life. He would make many mistakes as he matured, but God never turned away from him for one reason—he kept his heart soft toward the God. He loved the Lord with all his heart. David operated from his true self, not a false self. Discovering our true self allows us to feel safe enough to pursue true intimacy with God and maturity in our faith.

Questions for Reflection and Discussion

1. What do you need to do to discover your true self?

2. What are your first thoughts when you hear "When God thinks of you love swells in His heart?"

3. How did David live from the heart? What can we learn from his life?

And He said to her, "What do you wish?"
She said to Him, "Grant that these two sons
of mine may sit, one on Your right hand
and the other on the left, in Your kingdom".
—Matthew 20:2

Note to Reader: *I wish to acknowledge the extensive work that Dr. Paul Hegstrom, founder and president of Life Skills International has done regarding the truths written about mother-son bonding contained in this chapter. I first learned about this through Dr. Hegstrom, which is his copyrighted intellectual property. I am grateful that he has given permission to share these truths in this book.*

Overcoming Mother-Son Bonding — Repairing the Relationship Breach

Jason Bradshaw grew up in a middle-class home. He was the oldest of three kids and was the only son. His parents loved each other, but when Jason was twelve, tragedy struck their family. Jason's father was killed in a car accident. The family was devastated and Jason's mother grieved for several years.

As Jason got older his mother poured her life into Jason. He was the apple of her eye and she often saw her husband in Jason as he got older. "He looks much like his father," she thought to herself. His mother doted on Jason and sometimes Jason reacted to what felt like smothering to him. Jason's mother often prevented Jason from doing things that normal boys of his age do, for fear of him getting hurt or even losing Jason. Gradually, Jason began to feel controlled and manipulated by his mother. This developed into a love-hate relationship with his mom. On the one hand, he knew he was now the male head of the family and wanted to care for his mom, but he hated the control he felt.

Jason began to date girls as he got older and found that he sometimes masturbated to relieve the stress and pent-up desires he felt inside. He also found himself on the internet checking out pornographic pictures. He didn't know why he did this. He just thought it was normal for boys his age.

Jason went on to college and kept a distant relationship between him and his mom. He wanted to respect and care for her, but he wanted to keep his distance and gain his independence. Jason got engaged after college and things were great with his new wife. However, over the next several years he found that there was conflict in his relationship with his wife. Sometimes he felt the same feelings he felt when he was growing up with his mother. That feeling of control gave him a sick stomach. He often reacted to his wife when those feelings swelled up inside, "Stop trying to control me," he would say. His wife was surprised at these reactions as she was only trying to connect emotionally with Jason. She wanted to be a part of his life. Jason pulled away each time he felt these feelings.

When Jason and his wife visited his mom, his wife noticed that Jason's personality often changed when the three of them were together. Jason's wife felt like a third wheel. It almost felt like Jason was married to his mother instead of her. This caused arguments among them and Jason often demonstrated a very unloving spirit to his wife. Jason would always defend his treatment of his mother, often at the expense of his wife.

This pattern continued for many years into their marriage. Finally Jason's wife decided they needed professional help. Jason reacted negatively to the idea and felt the only problem they had was his wife kept trying to control him and she needed to stop. However, reluctantly, Jason agreed to go to counseling.

Jason, to his surprise, discovered in the counseling that the reason he reacted to his wife's "control and manipulation" as he perceived it, was due to something that happened in his childhood that related to his mother. The feelings he was feeling were the same feelings he felt when he was a teenager growing up. In essence, Jason was shocked to discover *he was subconsciously viewing his wife as his mother.* As the truth of his situation unfolded, Jason was able to recognize why he reacted to his wife this way.

Today Jason and his wife are happily married. However, many couples who have the same symptoms often result in divorce. The same scenario happens when a father divorces a wife. The mother is often left emotionally bankrupt and she seeks to meet her emotional needs from her son. However, a son is not made to emotionally bond with his mother and

> Many men never emotionally bond to their wives because of the impact of being emotionally bonded to their mothers during their adolescent years

the pain that is caused within him must be released through some form of sexual expression. That is one reason Jason turned to sex to relieve his emotional pain.

Compounded with this is the legitimate need for Jason to have an emotional connection with a female, but because of his negative perception of his wife, he often sought that emotional connection through women at his workplace or in other social settings. He was often seen as a flirt with women but Jason denied such behavior. This, too, is rooted in the mother-son bonding relationship.

There is a crisis in marriage today. Research reveals the Christian divorce rate is higher than non-believers. There are many reasons for this, but one of those reasons is rarely spoken about. It has to do with the inappropriate bonding between a mother and her son during his adolescent years.

Many men never emotionally bond to their wives because of the impact of being emotionally bonded to their mothers during their adolescent years. The reason many men are not able to bond with their wives is often due to mother-son bonding that takes place during adolescence.

Dr. Paul Hegstrom explains in his book, *Broken Children, Grown Up Pain*, that "a husband without an emotional bond to his wife sees her as someone who sleeps with him, cleans the house, takes care of the children, and works—he doesn't see her as a real, living, emotional person."[19] As a result, the husband is often distant emotionally to his wife, but he does not recognize this in himself. However, his wife definitely knows it. She tries to connect on an emotional level only to be perceived as trying to control him. This leads to conflicts in the relationship.

If the father and mother are not bonded to one another, the mother will often bond to the oldest son. This can happen as a result of an absent father, either physically or emotionally. If a wife is not getting her emotional needs met through her husband, she may attempt to draw this from her son. If the parenting style is weak in emotional validation, fails to give words of love, or shames the child, these combinations will eventually surface through problems in the marital relationship in adulthood.

Resolving an Inner Conflict

When mothers bond with sons during adolescence, the son rebels against this bonding because he is not wired to bond with any female once they get into adolescence without some form of sexual expression. When boys should be growing independent from their mother during this time, they find themselves in bondage to their mother's emotional control. This all happens subconsciously.

Gordon Dalbey, author of *Healing the Masculine Soul*, explains that "beyond the basic fact of initial physical dependence upon the mother, the quality of that bonding experience also influences the son's later relationships with women. If the boy's maternal bond was painful (perhaps his mother didn't want to conceive and thus rejected him) or inappropriate (perhaps she was seductive toward him), the boy may later associate physical bonding to a woman with pain and anxiety. He then may become compulsive about sex---either as the freewheeling playboy who is incapable of commitment, or the demanding husband who fears being emotionally vulnerable to his wife. Given the biological and emotional intensity of the mother-son bond, only someone whose intrinsic identity with the boy exceeds that of the mother can draw him away into individuality and adult responsibility. Clearly, only the father meets such a requirement."[20]

> If the boy's maternal bond was painful, the boy may later associate physical bonding to a woman with pain and anxiety

If unresolved, the young male will seek to rebel against this bonding and control they feel subconsciously. They will have a love-hate relationship toward their mothers during late adolescence. This can lead young males to masturbate or get into pornography or have premarital sex in their adolescent years as a means of dealing with the emotional pain of that bonding from the mother. The male will eventually pull away from the mother as a result of seeking to become independent from her. This can be traumatic for the mother.

These feelings are often felt subconsciously as the son grows into adulthood. Often an unconscious vow is made to themselves: "I will never be controlled by a woman again." This personal vow can go with them into future dating and marital relationships. The wife will often feel like their legitimate input is being viewed as criticism by the husband and he is resistant to talking with her at an emotional level. The husband will often shut down or rebel against his wife's input.

Dalbey explains that "when a boy reaches puberty, filled with the powerful physical stirrings of his emerging manhood, the father's role becomes critical. If at this point Dad doesn't call the boy out and away from the mother to bond with his masculine roots among men, those stirrings are overtaken by his natural bond with the mother, becoming bound up in her and thus unavailable later to the woman he loves.[21] Without the earthly father to call the son out into manhood, the boy grows up seeking manly identity in women – whose voices seem to call him to manhood through sexual conquest. Masculinity grows not out of conquering the woman, but only out of conquering the man – and not another man, as in war, but oneself."[22] Dalbey explains how this can further affect the man's identity: "Enmeshed with his mother, he may find that his heart is unavailable to another woman to walk with him later as a wife in his life calling (Genesis 2:24). Unable to bond with either a woman in marriage or a man in healthy friendship, he then may fall prey to homosexual impulses."[23]

> If Dad doesn't call the boy out and away from the mother to bond with his masculine roots among men, those stirrings are overtaken by his natural bond with the mother, becoming bound up in her and thus unavailable later to the woman he loves

This is why moral failure can happen even among the most mature Christian men. Despite a commitment to a disciplined Christian life, they have never resolved their inner toil rooted in mother-son bonding and eventually lose the battle. God's grace is needed to take the male back to the source of his pain to become healed.

Fear of Dependency

Paul Olsen, declares in his book, *Sons and Mothers*, "What a man is frightened of, more than anything else in the vast possibilities of living experience, is dependency, regression to a state in which he becomes an infant in the care of his mother — a mother later unconsciously symbolized by almost all women with whom he comes in contact."[24]

If the son has had any male to male sexual exposure in his childhood, this issue is compounded. Subconsciously he will seek to prove his heterosexuality by bonding to other women outside the marriage. When a dad abandons a son emotionally and physically, he is left to gain that validation elsewhere, often through a female or even another man. If the boy has any male-to-male sexual exposure he will grow into adulthood leaning toward homosexuality or he will have to prove his heterosexuality to himself by getting his validation from women.

The popular comedy TV sitcom series "Everybody Loves Raymond" is a classic portrayal of two sons who have been doted on by their mother and conflict consistently arises between the loyalty of the sons at the expense of their wives. The father is emotionally bankrupt and emotionally abuses the mother. The mother seeks to get her emotional needs met from Raymond, the favored son. Many of the situations are quite humorous, but sadly, are portrayed very accurately as to the depth of the problem.

Ken Nair, author of *Discovering the Mind of a Woman*, cited a perfect example of this when counseling a couple and the husband was reacting to his treatment of his wife. "I'm thinking of a situation where a wife said, 'On Mother's Day, you made sure that your mother got to sit at the head of the table and was waited on first.' He retaliated, 'Well, it was Mother's Day!' His wife defensively said, 'I'm a mother! In fact, I'm the mother of your children. But that doesn't seem to carry any weight with you!' He illustrated his deafness to her spirit by saying, 'I'm not going to stop loving my mother just to make you happy!'"[25]

This man always gave deference to his mother's needs at the expense of his wife's. The husband was never emotionally bonded to his wife, but was still bonded to his mother. When this happens the husband will pull away from his wife because he subconsciously views her as his mother who he believes is trying to control him. Whenever a son's behavior changes in the presence of the mother and the wife feels like a third wheel, you can be confident there is a mother-son bonding issue that exists.

Another reason that we are seeing more moral failure today is due to the fatherless generation that was ushered in through the baby-boomer generation

This usually results in the son bonding to other women outside the marriage in a subconscious attempt to deal with the pain of the mother-son bonding. He is often a flirt with other women usually unknowingly. Subconsciously he is meeting an emotional need in himself to prove his manhood through other women.

John Eldredge shares a very personal account of his discovery of similar deep rooted issues he described in his book, *Wild at Heart*. He discovered what happens when a man cannot offer himself emotionally to his wife. "If the man refuses to offer himself, then his wife will remain empty and barren. A violent man destroys with his words; a silent man starves his wife. 'She's wilting,' a friend confessed to me about his new bride. 'If she's wilting then you're withholding something,' I said. Actually, it was several things—his words, his touch, but mostly his delight.

There are so many other ways this plays out in life. A man who leaves his wife with the children and the bills to go and find another, easier life has denied them his strength. He has sacrificed them when he should have sacrificed his strength for them."[26]

The Father Wound

Another reason that we are seeing more moral failure today is due to the fatherless generation that was ushered in through the baby-boomer generation. Since the 1960's we have seen a steady increase in divorce and fatherless families. This has created an open wound in both men and women today.

Bill Clinton's sexual indiscretions with Monica Lewinsky in the White House brought shame to him, his family, and the nation. To make matters worse, he tried to cover it up by lying to the American people on national television, and later explained it away as "not being sex." Clinton will forever be remembered in the history books for his indiscretions. Gordon Dalbey explains:

"The shame from moral failure in men urges men into a variety of compulsive/addictive behaviors—from drugs and pornography to workaholism and religious legalism. In hiding his wound, the man eventually fulfills the awful impact of the Malachi 4:6 curse upon the land, from abortions and sexually transmitted diseases to crime and domestic violence. He's left fearful of women, distrusting of other men, shortsighted in

his view of God and, therefore, cut off from his desti-
ny. In a classic example, during the shameful exposure
of former President Clinton's sexual sins, few political
commentators noted that his father had died when
Clinton was in his mother's womb, and that his several
step-fathers were alcoholic and/or abusive. With such
a deep wound in his masculine soul and the constant
negative models at hand to fill it, the boy could only
grow up looking for security in the one constant re-
lationship, namely, his mother. He thereby learned to
seek confirmation of his manhood from women. But
since no woman is capable of doing that, and if he
never goes to Father God with his wound, he's con-
demned to the eternally fruitless exercise of going from
one woman to another seeking his manhood. The
nation has paid dearly for this with a skepticism and
even scorn for his leadership and authority. Certainly
Clinton must be held accountable for his choices and
eventually suffer their consequences. But—as destruc-
tive as the father-wound is—there's not enough brick
and mortar to build enough prisons to hold the men
who are acting it out. It's a deadly epidemic among us,
which hides in the shadow of shame."[27]

Tiger Woods

In December 2009 Tiger Woods' world went from a polished, protected family-friendly persona to a womanizer, shamed and gossiped about throughout the tabloid media due to moral failure and infidelity in his marriage. One of the questions that can often come up when someone like Tiger Woods, who seemingly had the world by the tail (pardon the pun), is "how could he ever want to go look outside his marriage with such a beautiful wife?"

Tiger fits the profile of a man deeply affected by mother-son bonding. Tiger is an only son. His parents divorced after he was an adult, but most likely the marriage had been weak for many years before the final divorce. It was well known that Earl Woods was not faithful to his wife.

Dina Parr, Tiger Woods' high school sweetheart, said in an interview that Tiger would call her crying, upset about his father Earl Woods' infidelity. Parr said Tiger would call her and say, "'My dad is with another woman' ... he would be so upset, so I just tried to be there for him

> If a son grows up in a family that fails to nurture him in his early years with appropriate touch, cuddling and affection, that child will grow into an adult with a greater sexual appetite in the marriage

and listen to him.'" Parr went on to say that Tiger loved his father, but he never really got over the unfaithfulness and that it's interesting that Tiger is now doing the same thing.[28]

We often saw Tiger and his mother together and the bond between them must have been very strong. This would have meant Tiger may never have really bonded with his wife Elin, and probably never dealt with the emotional pain from the bonding of his mother. This ultimately would have to lead to resolving the inner conflict in inappropriate ways sexually as he got older. Chances are that because Tiger never really bonded with his wife Elin during the marriage he sought to bond with women outside the marriage through sex.

Symptoms of a Nurturing Void

If a son grows up in a family that fails to nurture him in his early years with appropriate touch, cuddling and affection, that child

will grow into an adult with a greater sexual appetite in the marriage. He will associate sex with being loved by his spouse because
he was never touched growing up. He will want to be touched and
cuddled in the bedroom but will not want to be touched outside intimate times. He will find it difficult to give hugs, hold hands or give
healthy affection to his spouse. Sometimes a spouse may wrongly
conclude her husband has a sexual addiction because of his desire
for sex. If there is no pattern of pornography, he does not have a
sexual addiction in his life. He has a love and nurturing problem
that he never got as a child. Consequently, he will seek to have that
need met through his spouse. However, she can never adequately
satisfy his need. That's because it's a love need that requires healing
from his heavenly Father. Until that is met in him he will continue
to place pressure upon his wife to meet his sexual needs.

How Men and Women Deal with Pain

When there are emotional unmet needs in a relationship it can
lead to a breach in the marital relationship, and the husband
and wife learn to cope in two different ways. Larry Crabb has
summarized how both male and female use unique strategies to
avoid the deep pain when a failure in trust happens.

> *All of us are trapped by addiction to a desire for some-*
> *thing less than God. For many women, that something*
> *less is relational control. "I will not be hurt again*
> *and I will not let people I love be hurt. I'll see to it*
> *that what I fear never happens again." They therefore*
> *live in terror of vulnerably presenting themselves to*
> *anyone and instead become determined managers of*
> *people. Their true femininity remains safely tucked*
> *away behind the walls of relational control.*

More common in men is an addiction to non-relational control. "I will experience deep and consuming satisfaction without ever having to relate meaningfully with anyone." They keep things shallow and safe with family and friends and feel driven to experience a joy they never feel, a joy that only deep relating can provide. Their commitment is twofold: to never risk revealing inadequacy by drawing close to people and, without breaking that commitment, to feel powerful and alive. Power in business and illicit sex are favorite strategies for reaching that goal.[29]

What You Cover, God Uncovers

When Tiger tried to cover up his sin, he only made the humiliation factor grow in his situation. If he had been forthright by repenting in the beginning the level of humiliation would have been less severe.

If you are a believer and you live in compromise, you lose confidence in the faith dimension of your life. The Bible says we are to confess our sins one to another (James 5:16). The very act of bringing your struggle into the light brings healing. My friend Ford Taylor often says, "What we cover, God uncovers. What we uncover, God 'covers.'" If we try to hide our sin Satan has a legal right to humiliate us and will do so publicly. The more public a figure you are, the greater the humiliation. If you choose humility by initiating repentance, God will cover you by His grace and your restoration will be quicker.

Walls, motivated by fear to keep out further hurt, also keep out love

Why Won't He Talk to Me?

If the mother-son bonding remains unresolved, the negative behavior becomes a part of a man's personality at a subconscious level as he grows older. Until he is conscious that his behavior is abnormal, he lives in a world of independence, denial and conflict until he understands there is a problem. The wife struggles with thoughts and feelings like, "Why won't he talk to me? Why is he so defensive to my input?"

The way out of this is to come to the knowledge of the truth for the husband. The scripture says that *the truth shall make you free* (John 8:32). Men need God to heal their hearts of the pain in their lives that has been caused by this bonding and repent of the pain they caused their mates through their behavior. God will often force us into a crisis in our marriages to deal with the issue. The husband must deal with both the root and his behavior. He must acknowledge his failure to love his wife because the spirit behind this issue is an unloving spirit rooted in the mother-son bonding. He must actually tell himself "she is not my mother, she is my wife!"

Most men will not begin to change until they can understand the problem. It is not enough to complain to your partner that something is wrong. *Until the man understands the reason for the problem and the way to fix it*, he will not have the motivation to change. This is important because if our heart is not healed we will try to solve the problem through performance in order to relieve the pressure, but the root issue will never be healed. The temptation for men is to get their validation as men from their wives or other women instead of God.

There is another factor at play here as well. If a son grows up under a mother who is volatile and angry he will grow up fearing a woman's anger. The father often withdraws from his wife's outbursts, often abandoning the son to her emotional

> God will often force us into a crisis in our marriages to deal with the issue

fits. The son grows up fearing confronting any woman for fear of conflict and possible outbursts, and fears the woman will leave him. By succumbing to these fears the boy grows up to be a man who abdicates his strength to the woman. This can open the door to a "Jezebel Spirit" in the marriage. "Ahab" yields leadership to the woman in the home.

The solution to this is for the man to exercise his true manly strength through servant leadership. Usually the woman will resist his new strength at first because she will perceive it to threaten her control over the man. A godly woman must come to a place of recognition that she actually needs his strength and will ultimately desire more of this. An ungodly woman, who has simply replaced his mother in this scenario, will leave him.

A Word to Mothers

If you are a mother and want to know how to avoid falling into the trap of mother-son bonding, the key is to ask yourself a question as it relates to the way you relate to your son. *"Am I trying to get an emotional need met for myself by how I relate to my son, or am I trying to help my son grow up into a mature man?"* Often you will discover whether your relationship is healthy or not by simply asking this question. A mother must help her son enter into manhood. She must find ways that he can interact with other men who can help him develop into a healthy man. The Jewish bar mitzvah is a ceremony in the Jewish culture which recognizes the manhood of a young man by his father and community. It is a rite of passage every young man needs. The mother must let go of her son emotionally and encourage the separation to take place as he enters into his late teen years. If this happens, you will find your son will develop into an emotionally healthy male. Healthy relationships with other male figures are needed in the boy's life to invite him into manhood.

A Word to Adult Sons

If you are a husband/adult son and recognize that you have been impacted by mother-son bonding you must make some immediate changes. You have never effectively "leaved and cleaved" to your wife emotionally. You may or may not have to speak with your mother about this issue. However, you must begin to:

- *Set boundaries with your mother.* She must know that your wife is first priority in your life. This can be a difficult transition for many men because it will feel like you are betraying your mother, but you are not. You are cutting one unhealthy bond so you can love and emotionally bond to your wife.

- *Ask your wife to help you.* Ask your wife for input. Tell her to let you know when she is feeling like a third wheel in the presence of you and your mother. Your vulnerability will prove to your wife you are serious about changing.

- *Resist withdrawing emotionally.* Mother-son bonding creates a "feeling" of being controlled by your wife when she may simply be trying to connect emotionally. You will have to consciously say out loud to yourself when you have internal feelings that you feel controlled, "She is my wife, not my mother." Eventually those feelings will dissipate as you love your wife emotionally.

A Final Word to Men

The enormous increased level of dysfunction in our society due to absent fathers and broken marriages has ushered in a generation of adults who carry a lot of brokenness and pain. Men, it is important to recognize the subtle lie the enemy of our soul tells us. That lie is "I cannot live without her." We have elevated a woman's sexuality to the point of idolatry in our culture. The more you have been impacted by the mother-son bonding, the more you are prone to buy into this lie. Our source of strength cannot be the fair-haired woman; this can only be met by God if we are going to be Godly men. Healthy marriage can meet legitimate needs of both partners, but God must be our source for both spouses.

Questions for Reflection and Discussion

1. Describe the relationship you have with your mother or mother-in-law. Do you see any influence of a mother-son bonding issue? Explain.

2. Sexual issues can result from mother-son issues or a lack of nurturing during growing up years. Describe your relationship with your parents.

3. Transparency is the key to living a life of integrity. Explain the concept, "What we uncover, God covers. What we cover, God uncovers through humiliation."

No king is saved by the size of his army;
no warrior escapes by his great strength.
A horse is a vain hope for deliverance;
despite all its great strength it cannot save.
But the eyes of the Lord are on those who
fear them, on those whose hope is in his
unfailing love, to deliver them from death
and keep them alive in famine.
—Psalm 33:16-19

Overcoming the Performance Trap

One of the traps the enemy sets, especially for men, is the performance trap. Early in my childhood this trap was laid with the purest of sugar coating to ensnare me. I recall performing my weekly job of mowing the grass when one day I missed a few sections of grass. Mom promptly took me to the front yard and showed me where I had missed. Mom loved working in the yard and took pride in her yard. If I was going to mow her yard, it had to be right. I never missed a spot ever again. Even today I cannot mow my own yard and not have it perfect.

I was shy growing up. Mom and Dad thought I should get involved in sports to bring me out. I loved playing pickup football in the neighborhood. We always had the best yard for football. I was a cut above others my age. I was always picked first in the pickup games. After all, I played in the Gravy Bowl as quarterback and defensive halfback. I made a game winning interception in the Gravy Bowl.

Then came Little League Baseball. I started in right field and graduated to first base. My coach taught me how to throw and I began pitching. I became an All-star pitcher with a mean curveball for a twelve year old. I made the All-star team as a pitcher and pitched in the big game. My curveball was really working. I would aim for the batter and watch it cross right over the plate. At first the umpire called my pitches as balls instead of strikes because he thought they were going to hit him and the batter. He came up to me after the game and said he had never seen the amount of movement on a curveball like I was able to put on it.

Then came basketball. I played junior high ball and was moderately good. But it was not until I got to high school that I had developed into a good basketball player. I was in between sizes for a guard or forward at 6 foot, 2 inches. I often played both positions. I developed a deadly jump shot. My coach would put me out on a wing and get the

> We often derive our identity from the input our lives have on those that make up our audiences or circle of influence. This leads us to gain our validation from others instead of God.

ball to me. One game I scored 26 points and led scoring. When I was hot I could drop them from anywhere. However, I was slow and not a great ball handler so my jump shot was about it. We won the 4A state championship during my junior year.

Then came golf. When I was 11, I began to play golf. I first began caddying for my dad on Saturdays. Ten bucks for two heavy bags--$20! I was rich. Dad introduced me to the game and I was a natural. I loved the game and it became my sport. I lived on the golf course during summers, playing 45 holes carrying my golf bag on many days. By age 14, I had broken 70 several times and had three holes-in-one (golfers will understand the significance of this). I won all the junior tournaments in my area and at age 15 I qualified for the US Junior Amateur that was held in Boston, Massachusetts at Brookline Country Club where the US Open has been played. During the first two rounds, I played with Gary Koch who later played on the PGA Tour and is now a golf analyst for NBC. Ben Crenshaw also played in that tournament. Our high school golf team won the 4A state golf championship when I was a senior.

I say all of this, not to blow my horn, but to clearly establish the early childhood pattern of performance. Performance equaled value, validation and love. Because validation was not instilled through words or emotional intimacy growing up, I sought to gain it through my performance.

As an adult this translated into performance in business and in relationships. I performed subconsciously in the way I thought people wanted me to perform to gain love and validation. I mentioned in the earlier chapter that this is called operating from a false self, or poser. I struggled to experience the unconditional love of God. Intimacy in relationships was difficult. The bottom line was always performance, but this was subconscious and I could not recognize it on the surface.

We often derive our identity from the input our lives have on those that make up our audiences or circle of influence. This leads us to gain our validation from others instead of God.

In high school I came home one day after playing the last round of a high school golf tournament I was supposed to win. I was leading, but blew the last round. I choked. I took it hard and came home and shared it with my mom who did not know how to respond. I cried and felt like a failure. Instead of listening and explaining this was a normal part of life, she was not able to comfort me. From then on, I was never the same. I put more and more pressure on myself to perform which only made me tense up on the golf course. I would go on to get a full golf scholarship at the University of South Carolina. However, Satan destroyed that gift by making me live in bondage to performance. It was one of the first experiences I had with failure. Failure in golf would be the wound that would lead me to a decision for Christ at age 22.

God will always force us into our wound to destroy the lie that was spoken to us through it. It would be many years before I would discover that lie. That lie would allow me to sabotage many good things in my life. It would place me on a treadmill of performance that would create a false self that posed as THE "successful Christian businessman". Underneath, I would struggle to have intimacy with those close to me and with God. This was directly related to the wounds of childhood where I failed to learn or receive emotional intimacy. It wasn't modeled for me by my parents and I'm sure it was not modeled by their parents either. This wound will remain until God helps us recognize and heal that wound as adults.

It would not be until my mid-fifties that I would realize how deep-seated performance had impacted every area of my life. I had thought I discovered and dealt with performance 13 years earlier. However, there were more layers that had to be uncovered. I found that performance made me view others through my performance glasses. As a child, I lived under a self-imposed belief that I needed to perform to gain validation. As an adult this translated into a subconscious requirement on others to also have to live up to my performance standards. If you did not operate at a level of performance or excellence I expected, I would make it known, sometimes in direct ways, and other times in subtle ways.

It showed up in so many ways, from honking my horn at imperfect drivers, to having a bad attitude with a ticket agent who was taking too much time, to having a critical spirit in certain situations. It was subtle but tainted my view of the world. The internal, subconscious message was "if I must live under this performance mandate, you must also." I projected my life wound on everyone else. Now, it was not always that visible because I was a strong Christian leader who had discipline. So you might never see the invisible turmoil that was going on inside of me. This, too, was another form of performance. John Eldredge, author of Sacred Romance, says, "We choose anesthesia of the heart through some form of competence."[30] This certainly was the drug of choice for me.

Performance showed up in ministry in different ways as well. Although God did a deep work in this area and my writing reflected the deep work He had truly done, there were places where performance worked itself back into my ministry work. There were more layers to uncover. The more successful things became, the stronger the tendencies to have to maintain the machine. I was starting to have a divided heart that had a mixture of Spirit and performance. It is one of Satan's most devious and stealth strategies for the marketplace leader.

Satan always wants to get us to believe a lie about ourselves so we can live the smaller story of our lives. If we live our lives through our false self of performance, we are making ourselves an idol before God. Shame drives us to perform. "How long, O you sons of men, will you turn my glory to shame? How long will you love worthlessness and seek falsehood?" (Psalm 4:2). God deals with the performance idol by first allowing our performance to fail. That failure forces us to face the pain caused by that wound.

Once God shattered the performance, I began to invest myself into understanding the love of God in my own life and renounced the lie of performance Satan had been speaking to me. I began to discover the Father's love. This was not an easy process and took months to appropriate. Even this process was laced with performance temptations by thinking I could gain this by reading scripture and learning more "how tos". I'm still a work in progress.

One encounter of personally connecting with the love of the Father came through a mentor. I lost my earthly father at age 14 in a plane crash, so abandonment and rejection issues played into my performance issues. This man, in some ways, became a father figure to me.

> As Christians we often choose the path of performance to seek the Father's love and acceptance

He lives in another country. We were talking about my crisis at the time and he stopped midstream in our conversation and said, "Os, you must know something. I love you. I really love you. I believe God has given us a special kind of relationship. I just want you to know that."

I was taken by surprise at his comment and felt unprepared to respond. I said a respectful, "I love you, too. You have meant a lot to me." But there was no emotion behind the words because I did not know how to respond. The following day I was walking around a lake where I walk every day. My mind went back to the phone call and I began to weep. I wept for 30 minutes. The Lord was saying He loved me through my mentor. He reminded me that I had not heard those words from my father, even though I knew he did love me. He simply did not verbalize it.

I also realized the tendency to try to earn the Father's love through my performance. There is nothing we can do to earn

His love; we must simply be vulnerable enough to accept it. We don't get it by reading more scripture or DOING anything, it is something we must simply accept. We often refuse to be loved without working to be loved. We as humans require love to be earned. This has been our training. "The Lord your God is with you, He is mighty to save. He will take great delight in you, He will quiet you with His love, He will rejoice over you with singing" (Zephaniah 3:17). When the Father thinks of you and me He thinks of how much He loves us and how He will reveal Himself to us as we love Jesus. "He who loves me will be loved by my Father, and I too will love him and show myself to him" (John 14:21b). God chooses to love us through other human beings as a tangible expression of His love. God did that through my mentor that day. I've come to realize how important it is to verbalize our love to our children.

As Christians we often choose the path of performance to seek the Father's love and acceptance. I realized that because I had a distant emotional connection to my earthly father and lost him to an airplane crash at age 14, it was difficult to have a heart connection to my heavenly Father. As a result, performance was the bridge to that connection. It was the only thing I knew. John Eldredge, in his book Wild at Heart, shared a life-defining realization about his own lack of father connection.

He was attempting to fix a sprinkler system in his yard. Like me, John was not a handy man because he was never taught to be handy because his father was not around growing up. Yet, all of us men have a certain independence that we want to express by showing we are self-sufficient. After experiencing failure a few times during his project he realized it was surfacing anger that was not commensurate with the project. He realized something deeper was going on under the hood and he needed to discover what it was. He concluded the following after his experience.

I'd gone to bed with no resolution inwardly or otherwise, and bang—I was yanked out of a deep sleep at 4:00 a.m. to face it, and all my uncertainties. Wham— just as suddenly, I am hit with this thought: Get it right. *This is perhaps the defining vow or compelling force of my adult life: you are alone in this world and you'd better watch it 'cause there isn't any room for error, so* Get It Right.' *The detached observer in me says,* Wow—this is huge. You just hit the mother lode. I mean, jeez—this has defined your entire life and you've never even put it into words. And now here it is and you know what this is tied to, don't you? *Lying there in the dark of my bedroom, Stasi (his wife) sleeping soundly beside me, the broken sprinkler system lying in misery just outside the window by my head, I know what this is about. It's about fatherlessness. A boy has a lot to learn in his journey to become a man, and he becomes a man only through the active intervention of his father and the fellowship of men.*[32]

Without the earthly father connection to our lives, we are left with a void. That void can make it difficult for a fatherless child to connect with the heavenly Father at a heart level.

During this time, a friend gave me a book that was extremely helpful to me in my process of accepting unconditional love from my heavenly Father and other people. David Benner, author of *Surrender to Love*, helped me understand that "responsible behavior does nothing to increase the Father's love, nor does irresponsible behavior decrease it."[33] God loves unconditionally and desires us to experience that love at a heart level. He breaks this concept down more in his book:

> *The single most important thing I have learned in over thirty years of study of how love produces healing is that love is transformational only when it is received in vulnerability.*
>
> *Receiving love while he is trying to earn it will only reinforce his efforts to be lovable. Far from being transformational, this will only increase his efforts to earn love. And any love he receives will only be experienced as the fruit of these efforts.*
>
> *Genuine transformation requires vulnerability. It is not the fact of being loved unconditionally that is life-changing. It is the risky experience of allowing me to be loved unconditionally.*
>
> *Paradoxically, no one can change until they first accept themselves as they are. Self-deceptions and an absence of real vulnerability block any meaningful transformation. It is only when I accept who I am that I dare to show you that self in all its vulnerability and nakedness. Only then do I have the opportunity to receive your love in a manner that makes a genuine difference.*
>
> *Daring to accept myself and receive love for who I am in my nakedness and vulnerability is the indispensable precondition for genuine transformation. But make no mistake about just how difficult this is.*

> Responsible behavior does nothing to increase the Father's love, nor does irresponsible behavior decrease it

Everything within me wants to show my best "pretend self" to both other people and God. This is my false self—the self of my own making. This self can never be transformed, because it is never willing to receive love in vulnerability. When its pretend self receives love, it simply becomes stronger and I am even more deeply in bondage to my false ways of living.

How terrifying it is to face my naked and needy self—the self that longs for love and knows it can do nothing to manipulate the universe into providing the only kind of love I really need. The crux of the problem is that I cannot feel the love of God because I do not dare to accept it unconditionally. To know that I am loved, I must accept the frightening helplessness and vulnerability that is my true state. This is always terrifying.[34]

I was discovering how truly difficult it was to love myself unconditionally and to be vulnerable enough to let God love me unconditionally.

For the next several months I began reading and reflecting on scripture that described the love of God for His sons and daughters. I reflected on the love of God for me personally. Gradually I began to believe it and accept it. And experience it.

As the days passed from this time I began to notice something different. A lighter, less intense Os began to emerge. I recognized when the performance trap was being presented to me. I was more tolerant of others, not simply performing patience. I knew even that was a trap. I sensed a new lightness in my personality that genuinely wanted to connect emotionally with others. It was a different me that was beginning to emerge because Christ was healing the wound which was healing the heart. Others began to comment on what they were seeing. Comments that had words like "he's more relational now" and "gentler" and "fatherly" began to be said about me.

One of my first tests came through my daughter. "Hey dad, what are you doing tonight?" She was single and in her mid-twenties at the time and had her own condo. "Have you ever hung a ceiling fan?" Oh, when I heard those words I got a sinking feeling in my stomach. Oh, no! Not the dreaded ceiling fan! It immediately triggered feelings of past failure. I had hung many of these but had failed many times, getting frustrated and angry at me and everyone else. Here would be my test.

Growing up I was never good at household projects. When my mom asked me to do things, I attempted but always got frustrated and gave up. It was a source of wounds for me because I was never taught about household stuff. Dad was gone by the time I was 14. This became a source of frustration as an adult. I would revert to a child emotionally when faced with a household fix it job. Since my life was measured by performance, all this did was to show me how poor my performance was in this area which made me have a value of 0. I wrestled with my daughter's request; on the one hand wanting to help, but on the other hand knowing the risk.

Nevertheless, I took the challenge knowing this was my first test of freedom from the performance demon. I began slowly. We bought the fans and began. Early signs of failure began to emerge—wrong size screws! Back to the store we went. Midway I realized I had something out of sequence. I unwound my steps. Still at peace. "OK, I say to myself. Just stay calm and take your time." The project continued and continued and continued. Four hours later I completed the project. "It's done!" I shouted victoriously. And the best part is it works.

Now I am not ready to start a career in fix-it, but I am on the road to performance recovery.

God wants us to relate to each of us through a heart connection, not through our performance. Our motivation to obey should be rooted in our heart connection to our Heavenly Father.

I will give you a new heart and put a new spirit within you; I will take the heart of stone out of your flesh and give you a heart of flesh. I will put My Spirit within you and cause you to walk in My statutes, and you will keep My judgments and do them (Ezekiel 36:26-28).

Questions for Reflection and Discussion

1. On a scale of 1 to 10 with 10 being the greatest influence, what performance number best represents your life?

2. How much do you think performance plays a part in your belief that God loves you? Explain.

3. Why is being vulnerable with God and others key to experiencing the love of the Father?

And I will give you the keys of the kingdom of heaven, and whatever you bind on earth will be bound in heaven, and whatever you loose on earth will be loosed in heaven.
—Matthew 16:19

NINE

Overcoming by Transforming Your Past into a New Identity

Earlier we discussed that when Adam and Eve lived with God in the Garden of Eden they had intimate fellowship and communion with their Father. They ruled and managed the affairs of planet earth as sons and daughters. They were naked, yet unashamed. They experienced a level of love and acceptance no human has ever known. Every need they had was cared for. There was no sickness, no conflicts in their relationships; no selfishness, no crime, and the environment was always beautiful. It was God's world untarnished by sin. Imagine for a moment what a world without sin might have been like. It must have been incredible!

However, the moment they sinned they went from being God's favorite son and daughter to being orphans. There was a wall between God and them. Until that wall was broken down they could only come into His presence by sacrificing the blood of an animal. They were forced to hide behind their shame us-

ing a fig leaf. Only the priest could come into the presence of
God to sacrifice the life of an animal for their sins.

*Then indeed, even the first covenant had ordinances of
divine service and the earthly sanctuary. For a tabernacle was prepared: the first part, in which was the
lampstand, the table, and the showbread, which is
called the sanctuary; and behind the second veil, the
part of the tabernacle which is called the Holiest of All,
which had the golden censer and the ark of the covenant overlaid on all sides with gold, in which were
the golden pot that had the manna, Aaron's rod that
budded, and the tablets of the covenant; and above it
were the cherubim of glory overshadowing the mercy
seat. Of these things we cannot now speak in detail.*

*Now when these things had been thus prepared,
the priests always went into the first part of the tabernacle, performing the services. But into the second
part the high priest went alone once a year, not without blood, which he offered for himself and for the
people's sins committed in ignorance; the Holy Spirit
indicating this, that the way into the Holiest of All
was not yet made manifest while the first tabernacle
was still standing. It was symbolic for the present
time in which both gifts and sacrifices are offered
which cannot make him who performed the service
perfect in regard to the conscience— concerned only
with foods and drinks, various washings, and fleshly
ordinances imposed until the time of reformation
(Hebrews 9: 1-10).*

Then, behold, the veil of the temple was torn in two from top to bottom; and the earth quaked, and the rocks were split, and the graves were opened; and many bodies of the saints who had fallen asleep were raised (Matthew 27:51-52).

When Jesus died on the cross, immediate access to God was restored! No longer did we need a priest. No longer did we require the blood of an animal. Jesus was the bridge back to relationship and sonship. What a powerful picture of breaking down the wall of separation that existed for thousands of years. What a powerful picture of the love the Father demonstrated to you and I by this selfless act to remove the veil between us and God.

But Christ came as High Priest of the good things to come,[a] with the greater and more perfect tabernacle not made with hands, that is, not of this creation. Not with the blood of goats and calves, but with His own blood He entered the Most Holy Place once for all, having obtained eternal redemption. For if the blood of bulls and goats and the ashes of a heifer, sprinkling the unclean, sanctifies for the purifying of the flesh, how much more shall the blood of Christ, who through the eternal Spirit offered Himself without spot to God, cleanse your conscience from dead works to serve the living God? And for this reason He is the Mediator of the new covenant, by means of death, for the redemption of the transgressions under the first covenant, that those who are called may receive the promise of the eternal inheritance (Hebrews 9:11-15).

Thousands of years would pass before God would provide the remedy for man's sin. God chose to come to earth as a baby and to die on behalf of Adam and Eve's sin as well as every human thereafter. Luke 19:10 tells us "for the Son of Man has come to seek and to save that which was lost." Notice the word used in this verse is "that" versus who. Jesus reclaimed everything that had been lost in the garden which included 1) restoring their relationship with God as sons and daughters, 2) the authority to bring Heaven on earth as Jesus prayed, and 3) to enforce the more than 7500 covenant promises in the Bible on earth. And, like Jesus, they were to destroy the work of Satan on the earth just as Jesus did. We are now His exclusive, delegated representatives of Heaven on earth until He returns. He gave us the keys of the kingdom to unlock the prison doors of captivity that have kept you, me and others in a prison to habits, addictions, unforgiveness and a host of other sins designed to keep captive.

> God calls you and me to stand in the gap for the people and the culture. We are to exercise our authority to open prison doors.

> *And I will give you the keys of the kingdom of heaven, and whatever you bind on earth will be bound in heaven, and whatever you loose on earth will be loosed in heaven (Matthew 16:19).*

> *Then He called His twelve disciples together and gave them power and authority over all demons, and to cure diseases (Luke 9:1).*

> *Speak these things, exhort, and rebuke with all authority. Let no one despise you (Titus 2:14-15).*

God calls you and me to stand in the gap for the people and the culture. We are to exercise our authority to open prison doors.

So I sought for a man among them who would make a wall, and stand in the gap before Me on behalf of the land, that I should not destroy it; but I found no one (Ezekiel 22:30).

Jesus told the disciples that a new tool would be given them that would be a game changer—it was the Holy Spirit! It was like adding a star quarterback to a team that was already the best team in the land. It was like giving the fastest car on earth superchargers to increase its power by a hundred fold! Now it would not even be a fair fight with Satan!

Remember Satan's three greatest lies?

1. You are powerless over your circumstances,

2. You are a victim of an unjust God, and

3. He left you here to suffer.

All lies! We now know the truth. And the truth makes us free! (John 8:32).

In fact, Jesus says "You'll be even more powerful than me!" *Most assuredly, I say to you, he who believes in Me, the works that I do he will do also; and greater works than these he will do, because I go to My Father* (John 14:12). Do you understand what is inside of you and me!? The Holy Spirit!

Now what is one of our assignments as Jesus' representatives on earth? It is to destroy the work of Satan and set the captives free. *He who sins is of the devil, for the devil has sinned from the beginning. For this purpose the Son of God was manifested, that He might destroy the works of the devil* (1 John 3:8).

We are to execute His interests on planet earth. *"The Spirit of the Lord GOD is upon Me, because the LORD has anointed Me to preach good tidings to the poor; He has sent Me to heal the brokenhearted, to proclaim liberty to the captives, and the opening of the prison to those who are bound"* (Isaiah 61:1-3).

I trust you understand what God has done for you and me by providing Jesus as the bridge to our Heavenly Father through His death. And He has given us authority through the Holy Spirit as his "power of attorney" on planet earth.

Let's start opening those prison doors for those in captivity!

Questions for Reflection and Discussion

1. Jesus gave us the keys of the Kingdom. What do you think that means?

2. Explain Luke 19:10 and its implications.

3. Describe Satan's 3 greatest lies. How do we avoid being impacted by them?

"And you shall know the truth,
and the truth shall make you free."
—*John 8:32*

T E N

Overcoming by Realizing and Contending for Your Identity

ow that we understand the schemes of the enemy, we must now contend for what is rightfully ours. The moment we understand the source of attack and the lies behind them, we can begin a process of healing and victory. Jesus is our healer and deliverer. The very knowledge of our situation starts a process toward healing because the truth makes us free. The psalmist says "He heals the brokenhearted and binds up their wounds" (Psalms 147:3).

Often what defeats our lives is what we perceive to be true. Perception is not always reality. Our perceptions must be validated by the truth found in the Word of God. If you believe a lie about yourself, you will make choices based upon that lie. However, each of us must have a transformed mind. "And do not be conformed to this world, but be transformed by the renewing of your mind, that you may prove what is that good and acceptable and perfect will of God" (Romans 12:2). We must operate from truth about our situation and God's view of us.

Transform Your Past into a New Beginning

Remember, God always sees you in the light of your redemptive purpose, not your past failures or your present status. You are His workmanship created in Christ Jesus. The minute you let others define who you are, you make them an idol in your life. Jesus is the only one who has the authority to define you. Your identity is as a son or daughter of your Heavenly Father who loves you with an unconditional love. Experiencing this is crucial to being free.

Earlier we said that people get into addictions and seek to medicate their pain because deep down they want to know and experience the love of God. However, many do not believe He actually loves them unless they perform to gain that love. This is Satan's lie in an effort to place God's kids into religious bondage. Satan wants you to live as an orphan, not knowing or experiencing the love of your Heavenly Father. Addictions are imposters for love and intimacy.

Renewing our mind to the truth allows us to move toward

a healed heart. Knowledge alone does not heal. The combination of learning the truth about our lives and experiencing the Father's love and presence is how we become healed and begin to walk in victory and power over our past. Remember, we want to turn our past into a new beginning. It starts by renewing your mind and spending time in His presence. "You will show me the path of life; In Your presence is fullness of joy; at your right hand are pleasures forevermore" (Psalms 16:11).

If you experienced deep trauma from sexual or physical abuse you may need to work with trained intercessors or professional counselors to help you receive healing. God has His servants who specialize in such situations.

In my own journey I became free of performance, workaholism, shame, rejection and many other hindrances when I learned where these things originated. I had to close open doors by renouncing the root generational iniquity that allowed entry into my life and caused wrong beliefs that resulted in certain behaviors which manifested from them. God renewed my mind by learning to apply truth to my life situation.

> Remember, God always sees you in the light of your redemptive purpose, not your past failures or your present status

For example, I came to realize I was a workaholic and the root of that was fear of provision. This entered my life after the death of my father at fourteen years old. The life insurance policy did not pay off and so our family income was severely affected. During my 15-17 age years my mom would often say after I requested money for a need that "we don't have enough money for that." That became on open door for a lie that said, "It's all up to me. No one can provide for me but me. I'll never experience this again." This led me to work hard at anything I did to insure success. However my work was rooted in fear of not having enough. It's the same mentality of those who went through the Great Depression. They never want to experience that again so they often hoard their money in fear.

To counter this, I began working 40 hours a week instead of the 55-60 hours. That was a big change. It was my faith action required to defeat a stronghold and a habit. I was now saying "God, you are my source of provision, not me or my job. I trust You to provide. I renounce all fear and affirm You as my provider." I needed to tangibly demonstrate a change of belief through behavior.

Whenever something comes into your thoughts you must ask the question, "Who said that?" If it doesn't align with the Word of God, reject that thought. Speak to it audibly: "I reject that thought in Jesus' name." Cite the truth found in the Word of God.

That is what Jesus did. The devil came to Him during His forty day fast and tried to tell Him He could meet His needs and fulfill His destiny if He would only bow down and worship him. Jesus replied by saying, "Man shall not live by bread alone, but by every word that proceeds from the mouth of God" (Matthew 4:4). Jesus recognized that what Satan was saying was not from God. So, He rejected it and stated the truth audibly to Satan. Satan left Him after he realized Jesus was not taking his bait.

God wants you to be whole. He made you an overcomer.

"Yet in all these things we are more than conquerors through Him who loved us. For I am persuaded that neither death nor life, nor angels nor principalities nor powers, nor things present nor things to come, nor height nor depth, nor any other created thing, shall be able to separate us from the love of God which is in Christ Jesus our Lord" (Romans 8:37-39).

When you discover the depths and width of God's love for you, those hindrances will begin to take a back seat to your ultimate destiny. Paul prayed that you would experience this when he said: "... that He would grant you, according to the riches of His glory, to be strengthened with might through His Spirit in the inner man, that Christ may dwell in your hearts through faith; that you, being rooted and grounded in love, may be able to comprehend with all the saints what is the width and length and depth and height— to know the love of Christ which passes knowledge; that you may be filled with all the fullness of God" (Ephesians 3:14-19).

> The area that you gain victory over Satan will be the area you will be anointed to free others

Finally, let me say that the area that you gain victory over Satan will be the area you will be anointed to free others. God will use YOU in the lives of others because you have gained an authority in that area to free others. That will be your inheritance. The ancient Phrygians had a legend that every time they conquered an enemy the victor absorbed the physical strength of his victim and added so much more to his own strength and valor. So temptation victoriously met doubles our spiritual strength and equipment. It is possible thus not only to defeat our enemy, but to capture him and make him fight in our ranks.[35]

May you fulfill all God has designed you to be for His glory.

Questions for Reflection and Discussion

1. What does it mean to realize and contend for your destiny?

2. Is perception reality? Why or why not?

3. Explain the concept of an open door in your life and how Satan is able to influence you through that open door.

Notes

1. Dr. Paul Hegstrom , *Broken Children, Grown Up Pain*, Beacon Press, Kansas City, MO 2001,2006 p22
2. Craig Hill, *If God Is In Control then Why...?* Family Foundations, Littleton, CO 2008, p 185-189.
3. Barna Research, http://www.barna.org/faith-spirituality/260-most-american-christians-do-not-believe-that-satan-or-the-holy-spirit-exis?q=satan+realy, 2009.
4. C. S. Lewis, *Screwtape Letters*, Barbour Publishing, Uhrichsville, OH, 1992 p 31
5. Henry Wright, *Addictions*, Be in Health, Thomaston, GA 2007 p.5
6. Craig Hill, *Bondage Broken*, Family Foundations International, Littleton, CO 1987 P.7,8
7. Mike and Sue Dowgiewicz, *Demolishing Strongholds*, Boulder, CO p.24
8. Marshall Kirk and Hunter Madsen, *After the Ball: How America Will Conquer Its Fear and Hatred of Gays in the '90s* (New York: Plume, 1990) p 27
9. Gordon Dalbey, *Healing the Masculine Soul*, Thomas Nelson Publishers, Nashville, TN 2001, p 97.
10. Danny Wallace, 2012, www.DannyWallace.com
11. Craig Hill, *The Power of a Parent's Blessing*, Charisma Publishing, Chapter 4 pre-pub manuscript, Lake Mary, FL
12. Gordon Dalbey, *Healing the Masculine Soul*, Thomas Nelson Publishers, Nashville, TN 2001, p 151.
13. Dr. Paul Hegstrom , *Broken Children, Grown Up Pain*, Beacon Press, Kansas City, MO 2001,2006 p 48
14. Gene Edwards, *A Tale of Three Kings*, Tyndale House Publishers, Wheaton, IL 1980, p 39.
15. Dr. Paul Hegstrom , *Broken children, Grown Up Pain*,

Beacon Press, Kansas City, MO p 114

16. John Eldredge, *Wild at Heart*, Thomas Nelson Publishers, Nashville, TN 2001, p 150.

17. John Eldredge, *Wild at Heart*, Thomas Nelson Publishers, Nashville, TN 2001, p 150

18. David Benner, *Surrender to Love*, Intervarsity Press, Downers Grove, IL, 2003, p 77

19. Dr. Paul Hegstrom , *Broken children, Grown Up Pain*, Beacon Press, Kansas City, MO p 100.

20. Gordon Dalbey, *Healing the Masculine Soul*, Thomas Nelson Publishers, Nashville, TN 2001, p 20.

21. Gordon Dalbey, *Healing the Masculine Soul*, Thomas Nelson Publishers, Nashville, TN 2001, p 22.

22. Gordon Dalbey, *Healing the Masculine Soul*, Thomas Nelson Publishers, Nashville, TN 2001, p 81.

23. Gordon Dalbey, *Healing the Masculine Soul*, Thomas Nelson Publishers, Nashville, TN 2001, p 96.

24. Paul Olsen, *Sons and Mothers*, Fawcett Publishers, 1982 p 41

25. Ken Nair, *Discovering the Mind of a Woman*, Thomas Nelson, Nashville, TN 1995 p 146.

26. John Eldredge, *Wild at Heart*, Thomas Nelson Publishers, Nashville, TN 2001, p 184

27. Gordon Dalbey, *Healing the Masculine Soul*, Thomas Nelson Publishers, Nashville, TN 2001, p 151

28. http://blog.zap2it.com/thedishrag/2009/12/report-tiger-woods-father-earl-woods-was-unfaithful-too.html

29. Larry Crabb, *Shattered Dreams*, Waterbrook Press, Colorado Springs, CO 2001 p 95

30. John Eldredge, *Sacred Romance*, Thomas Nelson Publishers, Nashville, TN 1997 p 130

31. John Eldredge, *Wild at Heart*, Thomas Nelson Publishers, Nashville, TN 2001, p 227
32. David Benner, *Surrender to Love*, Intervarsity Press, Downers Grove, IL, 2003, p 20.
33. David Benner, *Surrender to Love*, Intervarsity Press, Downers Grove, IL, 2003, p 76
34. Source for ancient legend of Phrygians http://www.back-tothebible.org/index.php/component/option,com_devotion/qid,6/task,show/resource_no,13/Itemid,75/

Recommended Reading

See www.tgifbookstore.com

- *Change Agent*, Os Hillman
- *Change Agent Video Course*, Os Hillman
- *TGIF devotional*, Os Hillman
- *The Upside of Adversity: From the Pit to Greatness*, Os Hillman
- *Experiencing the Father's Love: How to Live as Sons and Daughters of our Heavenly Father*, Os Hillman
- *The Power of a Parent's Blessing*, Craig Hill
- *Healing the Masculine Soul*, Gordon Dalbey
- *Broken Children, Grown Up Pain*, Dr. Paul Hegstrom
- *Ancient Paths*, Craig Hill
- *Bondage Broken*, Craig Hill
- *Addictions*, Henry Wright
- *Two Dogs and No Flea*, Craig Hill
- *Listening to the Father's Heart devotional*, Os Hillman

Additional Resources by Os Hillman

See www.tgifbookstore.com

Change Agent: Engaging Your Passion to Be the One who Makes a Difference

Every person has a desire to influence others. Whether you are a CEO, housewife, student, manager or church leader, you have a circle of influence.

The Upside of Adversity: From the Pit to Greatness

Through a challenging seven-year process, Os learned that God was at work using these painful circumstances to prepare him for the calling God had on his life. So will you.

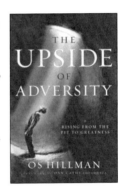

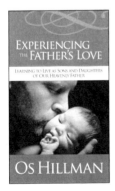

Experiencing the Father's Love: How to Live as Sons and Daughters of our Heavenly Father

When God thinks of you, love swells in His heart. Do you believe it? Os helps readers understand what it means to live as sons and daughters of our heavenly Father.

Listening to the Father's Heart devotional

What if you could eavesdrop on a conversation between God, the Father, and one of His sons on earth? Perhaps you might discover the heart of a Heavenly Father who loves all of His sons and daughters. Perhaps you would learn about His perspective on life. Perhaps something might be said that relates to your own journey to know the Father intimately.

FREE TGIF: Today God Is First E-mail devotional

Start your day by reading an e-mail that encourages you to experience the Lord's presence at work through this popular e-mail devotional that is subscribed to by hundreds of thousands daily. Subscribe by going to *www.TodayGodIsFirst.com.*

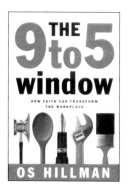

The 9 To 5 Window: How Faith Can Transform The Workplace.

Provides an in-depth look at this new move of God and how Christians can practically implement their faith with their work life.

TGIF: Today God Is First, Volumes 1 & 2

365 Meditations on the Principles of Christ in the Workplace. The daily e-mail devotional in book form! Today God Is First provides daily meditations that will help you focus your priority on knowing Jesus more intimately every day.

Making Godly Decisions

How can you know if you are making a decision that will be blessed by God? In Making Godly Decisions, you will learn the principles for making good decisions that are also godly decisions.

The Purposes of Money

Why does God prosper some, while others still live in need? Can we trust God to provide when we don't have enough? In this book you will discover five fallacies of belief that most people live by regarding money and the five reasons God provides us money.

Are You a Biblical Worker?

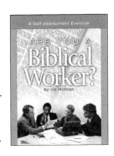

Here's a self-assessment tool to help you discover where you are in your biblical knowledge of applying faith in your workplace. The inventory test features fifty True/False/Sometimes questions and answers.

The Faith@Work Movement: What every pastor and church leader should know

Is there a real move of God in the workplace? If so, what do pastors and church leaders need to know? How can the church mobilize workplace believers to impact their city and nation? Os answers these and many more questions about the modern-day faith at work movement.

TGIF Small Group Bible Study

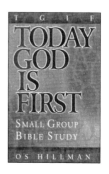

The popular TGIF: Today God Is First book is now a twelve-week, small group Bible study that is ideal for workplace groups. This study includes discussion questions and a workplace application with added scriptures that will allow the leader to extend or reduce the study time.

Faith & Work: Do They Mix?

When you have an intimate relationship with Jesus, you will understand that your faith and work are not separate in God's eyes. This book will help you understand why your work IS your ministry. Os provides a theology of work basis for bringing faith into your work life.

Change Agent Video Course and the Change Agent Intensive Weekend Workshop

This is Os Hillman's core workshop based on the Change Agent book. The weekend training consists of two and a half days and is limited to fifty participants. This workshop helps men and women discover their purpose in work and life, the six stages of a call for a change agent, seven-mountain strategies and much more. It is loaded with practical principles to understand God's method of calling, biblical decision making, and the role adversity plays in every believer's life toward becoming a change agent. Visit *www.marketplaceleaders.org* to learn more.

Become a Change Agent! Join the Change Agent Network

Each month receive in-depth biblical teaching on various topics related to your workplace calling, marketplace tips, proven business principles, teleseminars, webinars, and networking with other change agents, and free and discounted resources via this e-zine and online private membership-based website. Visit www.becomeachangeagent.com to learn more.

Visit Our Websites

- www.MarketplaceLeaders.org
- www.Reclaim7Mountains.com
- www.tgifbookstore.com
- www.UpsideofAdversity.com
- www.mlcommunity.com
- www.becomeachangeagent.com
- www.changeagentbook.com
- www.ChangeAgentVideoCourse.com

Marketplace Leaders • PO Box 69
Cumming, GA 30028 • 678.455.6262
www.marketplaceleaders.org • www.reclaim7mountains.com
www.changeagentbook.com • www.AslanGroupPublishing.com